Developing Listening Skills 2

Second Edition

Casey Malarcher

Compass Publishing

Developing Listening Skills 2 **Second Edition**

Casey Malarcher

© 2010 Compass Publishing

Acquisitions Editor: John Thomas
Illustrator: Hieram Weintraub
Design: Design Plus

email: info@compasspub.com
http://www.compasspub.com

ISBN: 978-1-59966-527-6

12 11 10 9
16 15 14 13

Photo Credits

All images © Shutterstock, Inc. except: p. 6 © iStock International Inc., pp. 13, 14 © Jupiterimages Corporation

Distributed By:
Grass Roots Press
Toll Free: 1-888-303-3213
Fax: (780) 413-6582
Web Site: www.grassrootsbooks.net

CONTENTS

36 Topics of *Developing Listening Skills, Second Edition*

UNIT	BOOK 1	BOOK 2	BOOK 3
UNIT 1	First Meeting	Entertainment	Locations
UNIT 2	Family and Friends	Shopping	Promises
UNIT 3	Free Time	Work	Special Occasions
UNIT 4	Date and Time	Computers	Steps and Plans
UNIT 5	Telephone	Travel	Music
UNIT 6	Directions	Restaurants	Groups
UNIT 7	Schools	Hotels	Outdoors
UNIT 8	Sports	Transportation	Meetings
UNIT 9	Appearance	Banks	Feelings
UNIT 10	Weather	Driving	Favors
UNIT 11	Instructions	Housing	Memories
UNIT 12	Stories	Health	Assistance

Entertainment

A

Look & Listen

Listen to the dialogs.

B

Listen Again

Listen again, and write the answer. ((Track 2))

1. How many tokens do they buy?

2. How did the man describe *Arena Fighters*?

3. What level did the man reach on *Block Builders*?

4. Where will they use their last tokens?

C

Essential Expressions

Sort the words and phrases into the right categories.

| show times | main menu | front row seats | high score | intermission |
| on stage | tokens | change channels | sold out | fast forward |

Video Arcade	Theater/Cinema	Television/DVDs

Listening Practice

A

How would you answer?

Listen. Write the answer. ((Track 3))

> $10 for adults and $8 for students.   That sounds like a good idea.
> At 7:45.   Let's play cards.   Not really.

1. _____
2. _____
3. _____
4. _____
5. _____

B

How would you ask?

Listen. Write the question. ((Track 4))

> Are any tickets still available?   Can you teach me how to play?
> Was it fun?   Do you like classical music?   When will the show close?

1. _____
2. _____
3. _____
4. _____
5. _____

C

Picture Description

Describe the picture using the words below.

> stage   seats   watch   performers

_____

_____

_____

_____

_____

✓ **Listen to the description of the picture.** ((Track 5))

Speaking Practice

In casual speech, you may hear the phrases "got to," "have to," or "has to" pronounced as "gotta," "hafta," or "hasta."

Written	Spoken
1. You've got to try this game.	1. You've gotta try this game.
2. We have to line up early to get tickets.	2. We hafta line up early to get tickets.
3. The singer has to be on stage for the finale.	3. The singer hasta be on stage for the finale.

✓ **Now practice saying the following sentences.**

1. Circus clowns have to wear a lot of makeup.
2. Everyone has to sit in the seat shown on his or her ticket stub.
3. I've got to watch the soccer game on TV this weekend.

✓ **Now listen and repeat.** ((Track 6))

B

Conversation Pictures

Listen to the dialogs, and number the pictures. ((Track 7))

✓ **Now listen to the dialogs again, and choose the correct location.**

1. (A) Balcony   (B) Front row   (C) Floor   (D) Anywhere
2. (A) Balcony   (B) Front row   (C) Floor   (D) Anywhere
3. (A) Balcony   (B) Front row   (C) Floor   (D) Anywhere
4. (A) Balcony   (B) Front row   (C) Floor   (D) Anywhere

Short Dialogs

A

Dialog 1

Listen to the dialog and questions. Choose the best answer. ((Track 8))

1. (A) It looks dangerous.   (B) It looks exciting.
   (C) It looks long.   (D) It looks old.

2. (A) Bad weather   (B) No money
   (C) Too many people   (D) Too scary

✓ **Listen again, and fill in the blanks.**

W: I want to ride that ❶_____!

M: The one with the double loops?

W: Yeah! Doesn't it look ❷_____?

M: Uh, sure. I guess. Uh, oh, look at the
   ❸_____.

W: It isn't that long. I bet we'll only have to
   ❹_____ fifteen or twenty minutes.
   Are you too scared to ❺_____
   this roller coaster with me?

M: I'm not ❻_____!

B

Dialog 2

Listen to the dialog and questions. Choose the best answer. ((Track 9))

1. (A) A bookstore   (B) A disco
   (C) A shopping center   (D) A theater

2. (A) A soft drink   (B) Milk
   (C) Fruit juice   (D) Water

C

Dialog 3

Listen to the dialog, and put the sentences in order from 1-4. ((Track 10))

_____ (A) He remembers when they rented the movie.

_____ (B) He suggests watching the previews.

_____ (C) She finds a DVD that they haven't seen yet.

_____ (D) She says he can change the channel.

Main Dialog

A

Listen

Listen to the dialog, and choose the best answer. ((Track 11))

1. Who did she see the parade with?
   - (A) A co-worker
   - (B) A friend
   - (C) A relative
   - (D) Her boyfriend

2. What does she like about the parade?
   - (A) The animals
   - (B) The clowns
   - (C) The food
   - (D) The music

3. Who is Mr. Fox?
   - (A) A millionaire
   - (B) A movie star
   - (C) A politician
   - (D) A pop star

B

Listen Again

Listen again, and fill in the blanks. ((Track 12))

W: Did you watch the ❶_____ yesterday?

M: Well . . . no, I was pretty busy. Did you get a chance to go?

W: Mm hmm . . . I went there with my ❷_____.

M: So, how was it? Did you both ❸_____ it?

W: We sure did. Actually, I go ❹_____ year, but this was my ❺_____ first time seeing it.

M: You're kidding me! You go every year? Is it really that ❻_____?

W: Oh, sure, it is for me! I really love ❼_____ to all of the marching bands and seeing the floats. This year, it was even more special. I got to ❽_____ Harry Fox.

M: The ❾_____? He was there?

W: Yeah, he was riding on one of the ❿_____ in the parade.

Short Talks

Listen to the short talk and questions. Choose the best answer. ((Track 13))

1. (A) An album   (B) A book
   (C) A movie   (D) A play

2. (A) The acting   (B) The directing
   (C) The music   (D) The plot

✓ **Listen again, and fill in the blanks.**

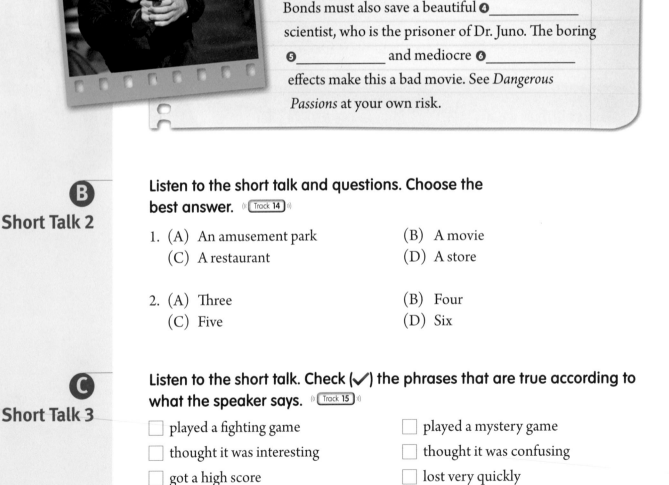

Dangerous Passions is the latest thriller by

❶_____ Roger Morrison. In this

❷_____, Jimmy Bonds, international spy

for the Canadian government, must save the

❸_____from Dr. Juno. And of course,

Bonds must also save a beautiful ❹_____

scientist, who is the prisoner of Dr. Juno. The boring

❺_____ and mediocre ❻_____

effects make this a bad movie. See *Dangerous*

Passions at your own risk.

Listen to the short talk and questions. Choose the best answer. ((Track 14))

1. (A) An amusement park   (B) A movie
   (C) A restaurant   (D) A store

2. (A) Three   (B) Four
   (C) Five   (D) Six

Listen to the short talk. Check (✔) the phrases that are true according to what the speaker says. ((Track 15))

☐ played a fighting game   ☐ played a mystery game

☐ thought it was interesting   ☐ thought it was confusing

☐ got a high score   ☐ lost very quickly

Listening Quiz

03:49

Listen to the dialogs. Choose the correct picture. ((Track 16))

A
Picture
Matching

1. (A)   (B)   (C)

2. (A)   (B)   (C)

B
Listen
& Choose

Listen to the dialogs and questions. Choose the best answer. ((Track 17))

3. (A) Buying theater tickets   (B) Going to the zoo
    (C) Playing a video game   (D) Watching a movie

4. (A) Five minutes   (B) Ten minutes
    (C) Fifteen minutes   (D) Thirty minutes

5. (A) A circus   (B) A commercial
    (C) A concert   (D) A comedian

6. (A) Art   (B) History
    (C) Science   (D) Sports

7. (A) The artist   (B) The beach
    (C) The colors   (D) The price

8. (A) Seats   (B) Singers
    (C) Theaters   (D) Times

9. (A) Buy a ticket   (B) Call an usher
    (C) Move seats   (D) Stay there

Wrap-up

A Pre-listening Discussion

Talk about these questions.

1. When was the last time you saw a movie? What was the movie?
2. When was the last time you went to a concert? Which concert was it?
3. When was the last time you saw a play? What was the title of the play?

B Listening Comprehension

Listen and answer the questions. Track 18

1. **How often did people report seeing live performances?**
   People reported seeing live performances ________________________.
2. **What was the most popular kind of live performance?**
   The most popular kind of live performance was ________________________.
3. **What reasons did people give for not seeing more live performances?**
   The reasons people gave for not seeing more live performances was ________
   ____.

C Dictation Practice

Listen again, and fill in the blanks. Track 19

When was the ① ________ time you saw a ② ________, a play in a ③ ________, or some other ④ ________ of live performance? In a ⑤ ________ of people 15 ⑥ ________ old or older, ⑦ ________ people said they ⑧ ________ saw one live ⑨ ____________ per year.

This survey included ⑩ ______ more interesting facts ⑪ ________ the habits of ⑫ ________ attendants. The most ⑬ ________ kind of live ⑭ ____________ to see was a ⑮ ________. About 50 percent of the ⑯ ________ who took the ⑰ ________ said they saw at ⑱ ________ one concert in the ⑲ ________ year. These concerts ⑳ ________ all kinds of ㉑ ________, from pop and ㉒ ________ to classical music.

A ㉓ ____________ small percent of ㉔ ________ said they attended a ㉕ ________, a musical, or the ㉖ ________ in the past ㉗ ________. However, it is ㉘ ____________ to note that the ㉙ ________ who did go to ㉚ ________ types of performances ㉛ ________ had higher education ㉜ ________ higher income than ㉝ ________ people taking the ㉞ ________. In addition, more ㉟ ________ went to these ㊱ ________ of performances than ㊲ ________.

Almost 75 percent of the ㊳ ________ taking the survey ㊴ ________ they would like to ㊵ ________ more concerts and ㊶ ________ events. However, they ㊷ ________ two factors were a ㊸ ________: time and money. ㊹ ________ did not have ㊺ ________ to go to a ㊻ ________ performance, or the ㊼ ____________ were not held at ㊽ ________ times. Also, ticket ㊾ ________ for live performances ㊿ ________ much higher than (51) ________ for other kinds of (52) ____________, like movies or (53) ________ sports.

Listening Test 🕐 08:29

PART I: Picture Description «(Track 20)»

Listen and choose the statement that best describes what you see in the picture.

1.

(A)   (B)   (C)   (D)

2.

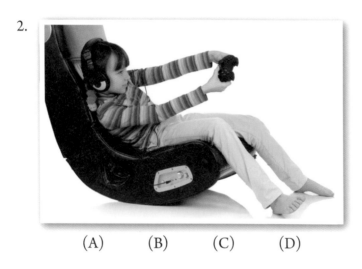

(A)   (B)   (C)   (D)

3.

(A)   (B)   (C)   (D)

4.

(A)   (B)   (C)   (D)

5.

(A)   (B)   (C)   (D)

PART II: Questions and Responses ((Track 21))

Listen and choose the best response to each question.

6. (A)   (B)   (C)

7. (A)   (B)   (C)

8. (A)   (B)   (C)

9. (A)   (B)   (C)

10. (A)   (B)   (C)

PART III: Short Conversations ((Track 22))

You will hear two dialogs, each followed by three questions. Listen carefully, and choose the best answer to each question.

11. Where are they?

    (A) At a museum

    (B) At an arcade

    (C) In a theater

    (D) In a video store

12. Who has played *Star Shooter* before?

    (A) Neither of them

    (B) Both of them

    (C) Only the man

    (D) Only the woman

13. What will they probably do next?

    (A) Play the fish game

    (B) Buy the DVD

    (C) Play *Star Shooter*

    (D) Push the start button

---

14. Where is this conversation taking place?

    (A) In a movie theater

    (B) On a roller coaster

    (C) In a kitchen

    (D) On the telephone

15. What does he probably want the woman to buy?

    (A) A ticket

    (B) A soda

    (C) Candy

    (D) Popcorn

16. What does the woman ask the man for?

    (A) His favorite flavor

    (B) His seat number

    (C) Some money

    (D) The size he wants

PART IV: Short Talks ((Track 23))

You will hear two talks, each followed by three questions. Listen carefully, and choose the best answer to each question.

17. What kind of show is being described?

    (A) A concert
    (B) A movie
    (C) A play
    (D) A television show

18. What is the speaker's opinion of this show?

    (A) It is boring.
    (B) It is exciting.
    (C) It is funny.
    (D) It is long.

19. What does the speaker predict about this show?

    (A) Few people will see it.
    (B) It will stay at the theater for a long time.
    (C) The cast will be famous some day.
    (D) The tickets will sell out quickly.

---

20. What did the professor study?

    (A) Adults who play computer games
    (B) Children and video games
    (C) Health problems from playing video games
    (D) The video game industry

21. Which statement would the professor agree with?

    (A) Children enjoy video games more than sports.
    (B) It is difficult to study violence.
    (C) Sports are more violent than video games.
    (D) Video games make kids violent.

22. Who disagrees with the findings of the research?

    (A) Children
    (B) Some people
    (C) The professor
    (D) The speaker

Shopping

Warm-up

A

Look & Listen

Listen to the dialogs. ((Track 24))

Fill in the blanks. ((Track 25))

...vorite _____ but not her _____.

...er _____ because the _____ are high.

...which _____ of her favorite _____ their grandmother has.

...er a _____ because her _____ are not that good.

...words to make correct sentences.

| ...teal | fake | flea market | children's department |
| ...sale | a deal | regular price | gift certificate |

...ricked and paid too much, he or she was _____.

...ch an item costs, look at the _____.

_____ at a store's customer service department.

...ch cheaper than expected, you might say it is _____.

...r a seven-year-old girl, look in the _____.

...r or used items at a _____.

7. If something...not real, it is _____.

8. The normal amount to pay for an item is the _____.

9. To buy something for less money, wait for it to go _____.

10. When you ask for a lower price because you are buying several items together, you are asking for _____.

A
How would you answer?

Listen. Write the answer. ((Track 26))

At 10 a.m.	I'm just looking, thanks.	On the fourth floor.
Size seven.	Yes, thank you.	

1. _____
2. _____
3. _____
4. _____
5. _____

B
How would you ask?

Listen. Write the question or statement. ((Track 27))

Are these the only ones you have?		How late are you open?
I'm looking for a winter coat.	How much is it?	Is this the sale price?

1. _____
2. _____
3. _____
4. _____
5. _____

C
Picture Description

Describe the picture using the words below.

baby	department	purse	towel

✓ **Listen to the description of the picture.** ((Track 28))

Speaking Practice

A

Pronunciation Practice

In casual speech, you may hear the phrase "let me" pronounced as "lemme."

Written	Spoken
1. Let me check the price.	1. Lemme check the price.
2. The store wouldn't let me return it.	2. The store wouldn't lemme return it.
3. Let me have a dozen.	3. Lemme have a dozen.

✓ **Now practice saying the following sentences.**

1. Let me call the manager for you.
2. The seller wouldn't let me have a deal.
3. Let me see that watch.

✓ **Now listen and repeat.** ((Track 29))

B

Conversation Pictures

Listen to the dialogs, and number the pictures. ((Track 30))

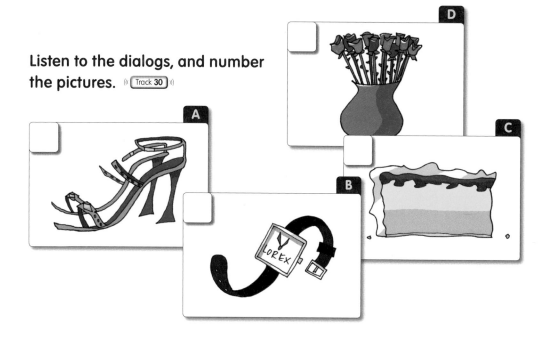

✓ **Now listen to the dialogs again, and choose the correct price.**

1. (A) $2.50   (B) $12.50   (C) $15   (D) $20
2. (A) $2.50   (B) $12.50   (C) $15   (D) $20
3. (A) $2.50   (B) $12.50   (C) $15   (D) $20
4. (A) $2.50   (B) $12.50   (C) $15   (D) $20

Short Dialogs

A

Dialog 1

Listen to the dialog and questions. Choose the best answer. ((Track 31))

1. (A) A friend (B) A relative
   (C) Her boss (D) Herself

2. (A) Candles (B) Candy
   (C) Flowers (D) Toys

✓ **Listen again, and fill in the blanks.**

M: May I help you?

W: Yes, I'm looking for a gift for a ❶_____.

M: Did you have anything in ❷_____ in mind?

W: I know she likes ❸_____. Do you have any?

M: Yes, they're right over here. The single ❹_____ are $15, or you can get ❺_____ together in one pot for $25.

W: I'll take the three ❻_____.

B

Dialog 2

Listen to the dialog and questions. Choose the best answer. ((Track 32))

1. (A) It is too expensive. (B) It is too large.
   (C) It is too small. (D) It is too tight.

2. (A) Less than $10 (B) Around $20
   (C) Almost $30 (D) Over $35

C

Dialog 3

Listen to the dialog, and complete each statement. ((Track 33))

1. The man paid _____ for a bag of _____.

2. He was ripped off because some of the _____ are _____.

A

Listen

Listen to the dialog, and choose the best answer. ((Track 34))

1. What is true about the shampoo?
   (A) It is expensive.
   (B) It is marked down.
   (C) The man likes its smell.
   (D) The woman likes it.

2. Which item is already in their basket?
   (A) Cookies
   (B) Eggs
   (C) Ketchup
   (D) Sugar

3. What does the woman prefer about cookies made from scratch?
   (A) The color
   (B) The flavor
   (C) The ingredients
   (D) The size

B

Listen Again

Listen again, and fill in the blanks. ((Track 35))

M: We should finish shopping soon. Why are we stopping here?

W: Look at this. I've never used this kind of ❶_____, but it's on sale. Should we try it?

M: Sure. That's fine with me.

W: OK, so it looks like we're pretty much done. Did we get ❷_____ on our shopping list?

M: Let me check it one more time. You got ❸_____, didn't you?

W: Yes, it's ❹_____ here.

M: It looks like we've got everything except ❺_____.

W: Oh, that reminds me. We need to buy ❻_____ so I can make ❼_____.

M: Do we really need to get it now? Why do you ❽_____ to make them when we can just ❾_____ them?

W: Homemade cookies ❿_____ better, don't you think?

Short Talks

A

Short Talk 1

Listen to the short talk and questions. Choose the best answer. ((Track 36))

1. (A) Brand-new ones
   (C) Expensive ones

   (B) Damaged ones
   (D) Old ones

2. (A) All week
   (C) Saturday and Sunday

   (B) Monday through Friday
   (D) Only at night

✓ **Listen again, and fill in the blanks.**

If you are interested in buying used goods at a low price, you should shop at a ❶_____ market. Usually flea markets are open on ❷_____, but in some areas they are only open once or twice a ❸_____. It is fun to walk around at a flea market and talk to the people ❹_____ things. It can also be fun to try and get a ❺_____ price on ❻_____ you find there.

B

Short Talk 2

Listen to the short talk and questions. Choose the best answer. ((Track 37))

1. (A) Hats
   (B) Jackets
   (C) Purses
   (D) Underwear

2. (A) Fifteen minutes
   (B) Half an hour
   (C) An hour
   (D) All day

C

Short Talk 3

Listen to the short talk, and write T for true or F for false for each statement. ((Track 38))

1. _____ The speaker knows his cousin's favorite color.

2. _____ The speaker knows his cousin's favorite superhero.

3. _____ The speaker bought a superhero T-shirt for his cousin.

Listening Quiz 04:06

A

Picture Matching

Listen to the dialogs. Choose the correct picture. ((Track 39))

A

B

C

1. (A)   (B)   (C)

2. (A)   (B)   (C)

B

Listen & Choose

Listen to the dialogs and questions. Choose the best answer. ((Track 40))

3. (A) Cashier   (B) Chef
   (C) Model   (D) Salesperson

4. (A) A different size   (B) Another brand
   (C) Other foods   (D) Plates and cups

5. (A) She doesn't like the color.   (B) She forgot her purse.
   (C) She got the wrong change.   (D) She needs another size.

6. (A) A computer   (B) Books
   (C) Clothes   (D) Food

7. (A) It is normal.   (B) It is leather.
   (C) It is too high.   (D) It is too low.

8. (A) It is handmade.   (B) It is broken.
   (C) It is damaged.   (D) It is small.

9. (A) Return it   (B) Look in another store
   (C) Buy it   (D) Ask for a lower price

Wrap-up

A
Pre-listening Discussion

Talk about these questions.

1. Where is your favorite place to go shopping?
2. What special services does this place offer?
3. Have you been to a mall with an ice rink or amusement rides in it? If so, where?

B
Listening Comprehension

Listen and answer the questions. ((Track 41))

1. **In which country and city is this mall located?**
   This mall is located in _____.

2. **How many other attractions besides shopping are described in this mall?**
   Besides shopping, _____ other attractions are described in this mall.

3. **Which has more rides, the amusement park or the water park?**
   _____ has more rides.

C
Dictation Practice

Listen again, and fill in the blanks. ((Track 42))

Some people enjoy ❶_____ to see amazing ❷_____ areas or enjoy ❸_____ activities that are ❹_____ for that area. ❺_____ people like to ❻_____ to go shopping ❼_____ a place where ❽_____ shopping can be ❾____ unique and exciting ❿_____. If you like ⓫_____, for the ultimate ⓬_____ experience, you should ⓭_____ the West Edmonton ⓮_____ in Canada. This mall ⓯_____ more than 480,000 ⓰_____ meters, which is about the ⓱_____ of forty-eight city ⓲_____!

Inside the mall, there ⓳_____ plenty of things to ⓴_____ shoppers happy. Along with ㉑_____ major department stores, ㉒_____ mall has over ㉓_____ other stores and ㉔_____. In addition, the ㉕_____ offers attractions not ㉖_____ found in other ㉗_____ malls.

One of the ㉘_____ attractions at West Edmonton ㉙_____ is an amusement park with ㉚_____ rides, including a fourteen-story triple ㉛_____ roller coaster. Or for ㉜_____ who prefer water, ㉝_____ is also a ㉞_____ park inside the mall, with ㉟_____ rides and slides. ㊱_____ lovers can enjoy ㊲_____ indoor salt-water ㊳_____. One lake is the ㊴_____ of a family of ㊵_____, hundreds of tropical ㊶_____, a sea turtle, and ㊷_____ sea life. The other ㊸_____ has many different ㊹_____ of tropical fish ㊺_____ a real coral reef ㊻_____ in it! To ㊼_____ the best view of the ㊽_____, shoppers can ride in a ㊾_____ submarine through the ㊿_____. The mall also 51_____ an ice skating rink and a 52_____ golf course, all under 53_____ roof.

With all of 54_____ to offer, it is not 55_____ that West Edmonton Mall is the 56_____ popular tourist attraction in 57_____.

Listening Test

PART I: Picture Description ((Track 43))

Listen and choose the statement that best describes what you see in the picture.

1.

(A)   (B)   (C)   (D)

2.

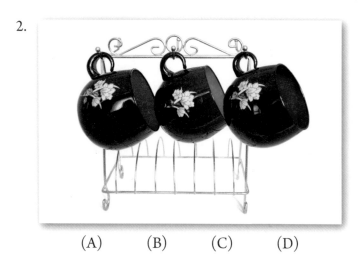

(A)   (B)   (C)   (D)

3.

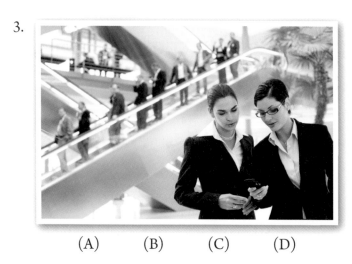

(A)   (B)   (C)   (D)

4.

(A)   (B)   (C)   (D)

5.

(A)   (B)   (C)   (D)

PART II: Questions and Responses ((Track 44))

Listen and choose the best response to each question.

6. (A)   (B)   (C)

7. (A)   (B)   (C)

8. (A)   (B)   (C)

9. (A)   (B)   (C)

10. (A)   (B)   (C)

PART III: Short Conversations ((Track 45))

You will hear two dialogs, each followed by three questions. Listen carefully, and choose the best answer to each question.

11. What does the woman want to buy?

    (A) A novel
    (B) A play
    (C) An electronics kit
    (D) A newspaper

12. What problem did the woman have?

    (A) She didn't want to be there.
    (B) She didn't have any money.
    (C) She was in a hurry.
    (D) She already had the best seller.

13. What did the salesperson finally suggest?

    (A) To buy the author's first book
    (B) To meet the author
    (C) To figure out what she wants to buy
    (D) To buy a new car

---

14. Which is true about the gift?

    (A) It's for his girlfriend's birthday.
    (B) It's a book.
    (C) His girlfriend did not like it.
    (D) It's for Valentine's Day.

15. What did the man's friend suggest?

    (A) Get a different gift
    (B) Buy two gifts
    (C) Return the gift quickly
    (D) Talk to his girlfriend

16. What was the man's explanation?

    (A) He wants to save money to buy another gift.
    (B) She likes chocolates.
    (C) It won't bother her.
    (D) He wants to travel.

PART IV: Short Talks ((Track 46))

You will hear two talks, each followed by three questions. Listen carefully, and choose the best answer to each question.

17. What does this announcement tell shoppers?

   (A) It is almost closing time.
   (B) A child is lost.
   (C) The supermarket is very busy.
   (D) There is a big sale in the camera department.

18. Where should shoppers go?

   (A) To the camera department
   (B) To the cashiers
   (C) To the customer service center
   (D) To the snack bar

19. How much time did shoppers have?

   (A) Fifteen minutes
   (B) Forty-five minutes
   (C) Fifty minutes
   (D) There is no time.

---

20. What does this ad remind shoppers about?

   (A) The coming holidays
   (B) The importance of a good diet
   (C) The things children enjoy
   (D) The weekend

21. What does Tina's sell?

   (A) Pets
   (B) Music
   (C) Food
   (D) Toys

22. Which of these are good at Tina's?

   (A) Customer service and selection
   (B) Price and customer service
   (C) Store atmosphere
   (D) Selection and price

Work

GET A JOB

Warm-up

Listen to the dialogs. (((Track 47)))

Listen again, and circle the right word or phrase. (((Track 48)))

1. He thinks she will be a good (veterinarian / trainer) because she likes animals.
2. He wanted to be an (action star / actor), but he didn't think he could really make a living.
3. He thought she would make a good lawyer because she likes to (write / argue).
4. He would really like to be a (publisher / writer), but now he just writes for fun.

Match the word or phrase to the right definition.

1. benefits •
2. customers •
3. deadline •
4. hiring •
5. make a living •
6. part-time •
7. responsibilities •
8. résumé •
9. salary •
10. starting position •

• (A) A low or first level job
• (B) Earn enough money to pay for what you need to live
• (C) Looking for someone to do a job
• (D) The money you earn for your job
• (E) Working less than forty hours per week
• (F) The people who use a service or buy a product
• (G) Written information about your education and experience
• (H) The things you have to do for work
• (I) The time or date when something has to be done
• (J) Things like health insurance, paid vacations, a retirement plan, etc.

Listening Practice

A

How would you answer?

Listen. Write the answer. ((Track 49))

> I work in a coffee shop.   Just part-time.   It's great!
> About two and a half years.   I'm a computer programmer.

1. _____
2. _____
3. _____
4. _____
5. _____

B

How would you ask?

Listen. Write the question. ((Track 50))

> How many hours do you work each week?   How much vacation time do you get?
> Do you enjoy your job?   Is the salary good?   What time do you finish work?

1. _____
2. _____
3. _____
4. _____
5. _____

C

Picture Description

Describe the picture using the words below.

| veterinarian | examine | wear | listen |

✓ **Listen to the description of the picture.** ((Track 51))

Speaking Practice

A

Intonation Practice

In certain three-syllable statements or questions, the stress should be on the last syllable. Say the following statements and questions using the stress pattern "dum dum da."

Written	Spoken
1. He's the boss.	1. He's the **boss**.
2. How's your job?	2. How's your **job**?
3. Who is he?	3. Who is **he**?

✓ **Now practice saying the following sentences. Remember to stress the last syllable.**

1. Was it fun?
2. Need a job?
3. Put it here.

✓ **Now listen and repeat.** ((Track 52))

B

Conversation Pictures

Listen to the dialogs, and number the pictures. ((Track 53))

✓ **Now listen to the dialogs again, and choose the correct time of each activity.**

1. (A) Fifteen   (B) High school   (C) Freshman   (D) Through college
2. (A) Fifteen   (B) High school   (C) Freshman   (D) Through college
3. (A) Fifteen   (B) High school   (C) Freshman   (D) Through college
4. (A) Fifteen   (B) High school   (C) Freshman   (D) Through college

Short Dialogs

Dialog 1

Listen to the dialog and questions. Choose the best answer. ((Track 54))

1. (A) Accepting his payment
   (C) Interviewing him
   (B) Buying a gift
   (D) Complaining about a product

2. (A) Every day
   (C) Sometimes
   (B) Most of the time
   (D) Never

✓ **Listen again, and fill in the blanks.**

W: Do you have any experience in ❶_____ service?

M: That was one of my ❷_____ responsibilities when I worked in K&C's Department Store.

W: I see. Did you have to ❸_____ many customers' complaints?

M: From ❹_____. But at K&C's, we were taught "the customer is always ❺_____." So we did our best to ❻_____ our customers' needs.

W: We have that same policy in our stores.

B

Dialog 2

Listen to the dialog and questions. Choose the best answer. ((Track 55))

1. (A) Growing plants
   (C) Serving food
   (B) Driving
   (D) Writing

2. (A) Cleaning hotel rooms
   (C) Serving ice cream
   (B) Selling books
   (D) Washing cars

C

Dialog 3

Listen to the dialog, and check (✔) the information that can be inferred from what is said. ((Track 56))

1. ☐ The job's pay is low.
   ☐ The job's pay is quite good.

2. ☐ She is a low-level employee.
   ☐ She is a manager.

Main Dialog

A

Listen

Listen to the dialog, and choose the best answer. ((Track 57))

1. What is the woman probably going to do?
   - (A) Apply for a job
   - (B) Start a company
   - (C) Take a class
   - (D) Write an article

2. What is the first thing the man listed?
   - (A) Jobs
   - (B) Hobbies and interests
   - (C) Goals
   - (D) School and degrees

3. Which might be listed in the last part of the résumé?
   - (A) Her income
   - (B) Her present job
   - (C) A college degree
   - (D) A scholarship

B

Listen Again

Listen again, and fill in the blanks. ((Track 58))

W: Could you help me with my résumé?

M: Sure. What kind of ❶_____ do you need?

W: Well . . . what do you think I should ❷_____ first?

M: On my résumé, I listed my ❸_____ first.

W: After that, do you put your ❹_____ experience?

M: Mm hmm, that's right. But there's something that you might want to keep in mind. Make sure that you list your past ❺_____ going backwards in time from your ❻_____ one to your first one.

W: That sounds easy enough, but what do you think I should ❼_____ on my résumé after that?

M: Well, it depends. ❽_____ people put other kinds of experience or ❾_____ they have received.

W: OK, sounds great. Thanks. These suggestions are really ❿_____.

RÉSUMÉ

CAREER SUMMARY

18 years in civil design and ce
structural designer in consulti
commercial building and cemen
gas industry thru. Currently ass
ongoing project Greenfield Area.

Familiar with ACI, AISC, AS
ISCP Sta

Short Talks

A
Short Talk 1

Listen to the short talk and questions. Choose the best answer. ((Track 59))

1. (A) Make clothing
   (C) Sell advertisements
   (B) Teach reading and writing
   (D) Work with computers

2. (A) One day
   (C) Ten days
   (B) One week
   (D) Two months

✓ **Listen again, and fill in the blanks.**

Do you want an exciting job working with
❶_____? Info Dex is now looking for young
people to work in ❷_____ positions with our
company. After a ❸_____ training period, you
can begin your new career in the ❹_____ field.
For more information on this ❺_____ opportunity,
❻_____ Info Dex at 888-INFODEX.

B
Short Talk 2

Listen to the short talk and questions. Choose the best answer. ((Track 60))

1. (A) It's boring.
   (C) It's great.
   (B) It's exciting.
   (D) It's not good.

2. (A) Art
   (C) English
   (B) Business
   (D) Social work

C
Short Talk 3

Listen to the short talk, and circle the jobs that the speaker mentions. ((Track 61))

apartment manager

cleaning person

landscaper

computer programmer

lawyer

college professor

Listening Quiz 04:09

Listen to the dialogs. Choose the correct picture. ((Track 62))

| A | B | C |

1. (A)　　　　(B)　　　　(C)

2. (A)　　　　(B)　　　　(C)

B

Listen & Choose

Listen to the dialogs and questions. Choose the best answer. ((Track 63))

3. (A) He is good at history.　　　　(B) Doctors work long hours.
   (C) The clients are healthy.　　　　(D) Lawyers make more money.

4. (A) All the time　　　　(B) Usually
   (C) Sometimes　　　　(D) Never

5. (A) It's a good company.　　　　(B) It's a new company.
   (C) It's a small company.　　　　(D) It's a terrible company.

6. (A) Bonus pay　　　　(B) Insurance
   (C) Vacation time　　　　(D) Working schedules

7. (A) Her job　　　　(B) Her company's product
   (C) How she goes to work　　　　(D) Where she works

8. (A) A summer job　　　　(B) Future careers
   (C) His brother's job　　　　(D) How to get a job

9. (A) Answer the phone　　　　(B) Carry packages
   (C) Cook food　　　　(D) Fix cars

Wrap-up

Talk about these questions.

1. Which occupations have the best salaries?
2. Which occupations have the best working conditions?
3. What education do you need for the jobs you listed above?

Listen and answer the questions. ((Track 64))

1. **Which occupation is the fastest growing field for people with professional degrees?**
   The fastest growing occupation for people with professional degrees is

   _____.

2. **What level of education do speech therapists need?**
   Speech therapists need a _____.

3. **What kinds of jobs can people with associate degrees find?**
   People with associate degrees can find jobs as _____

   _____.

Listen again, and fill in the blanks. ((Track 65))

Are there some ❶_____ that have more ❷_____ opportunities than others? A government ❸_____ in the United States ❹_____ jobs to find the ❺_____ growing occupations. The agency ❻_____ the occupations according to the ❼_____ of education people ❽_____ for the jobs. Four ❾_____ of education ❿___ this research were professional, ⓫_____, bachelor, and associate degrees. ⓬_____ to those levels, here ⓭_____ the results that the ⓮_____ found.

Let's look at people getting professional ⓯_____ in university. For this group, the fastest growing ⓰_____ is that of veterinarian. Another fast-⓱_____ occupation is that of ⓲_____. Of course, lots of ⓳_____ with professional degrees are ⓴_____ and lawyers. However, in these fields, jobs ㉑_____ becoming harder to ㉒_____.

As for those with ㉓_____ degrees, more and more ㉔_____ graduates are entering the ㉕_____ of computer research and ㉖_____ research. No doubt this is ㉗_____ to the rapid growth ㉘___ the Internet over the ㉙_____ decade. Many students graduating ㉚_____ master's degrees are entering the ㉛_____ of speech therapy and social ㉜_____.

Most people who ㉝_____ a bachelor's degree and ㉞_____ work experience are finding ㉟_____ in businesses as managers. The ㊱_____ growing fields for these ㊲_____ are in positions like ㊳_____ system managers or advertising and ㊴_____ managers.

There are also ㊵_____ jobs available for people ㊶_____ have associate degrees. Many ㊷_____ with this type of ㊸_____ are finding jobs such as ㊹_____ support specialists, physical therapists, and ㊺_____ technicians.

Listening Test ^{08:30} 🕐

PART I: Picture Description ((Track 66))

Listen and choose the statement that best describes what you see in the picture.

1.

(A)　　(B)　　(C)　　(D)

2.

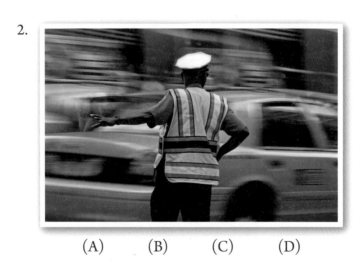

(A)　　(B)　　(C)　　(D)

3.

(A)　　(B)　　(C)　　(D)

4.

(A)   (B)   (C)   (D)

5.

(A)   (B)   (C)   (D)

PART II: Questions and Responses ((Track 67))

Listen and choose the best response to each question.

6. (A)   (B)   (C)

7. (A)   (B)   (C)

8. (A)   (B)   (C)

9. (A)   (B)   (C)

10. (A)   (B)   (C)

PART III: Short Conversations ((Track 68))

You will hear two dialogs, each followed by three questions. Listen carefully, and choose the best answer to each question.

11. What does the man assume about the woman?

    (A) She is a doctor.

    (B) She enjoys her job.

    (C) She is single.

    (D) She will retire soon.

12. What did the woman say about her job?

    (A) It is very satisfying.

    (B) She doesn't like her job.

    (C) She enjoys working.

    (D) She's always busy.

13. What did the man say that the woman agreed with?

    (A) Her job is dangerous.

    (B) She is very tired.

    (C) She takes long vacations.

    (D) She works many hours.

---

14. What question is the woman asked?

    (A) What time does she like to finish work?

    (B) What are her hobbies?

    (C) What kind of food does she enjoy?

    probably finish work today?

    have to do after she finishes work?

    th her friend

    with her boss

    nt is made about the woman's plans?

    It's nice of her to be invited for dinner.

    (B) She should get out more.

    (C) She will finish work at six today.

    (D) She should eat more vegetables.

PART IV: Short Talks ((Track 69))

You will hear two talks, each followed by three questions. Listen carefully, and choose the best answer to each question.

17. What is the benefit being described?

  (A) Choosing working hours
  (B) Flexible managers
  (C) Medical insurance
  (D) Working at home

18. Why does the speaker work longer hours?

  (A) To make extra money
  (B) Because she is a manager
  (C) Because she works two jobs
  (D) So she doesn't have to work every Friday.

19. What does the speaker say you are not required to do?

  (A) Work on weekends
  (B) Wake up early
  (C) Work long hours
  (D) Work from nine to five each day

---

20. What was the target market for his father's business?

  (A) Children
  (B) College students
  (C) Single adults
  (D) The speaker does not say.

21. Which is true of his father's company?

  (A) It closed.
  (B) It is still in business.
  (C) It now employs millions of people.
  (D) It took over his previous company.

22. What is the speaker's opinion of his father's company?

  (A) He thinks his father's plans worked well.
  (B) He wishes his father didn't start the company.
  (C) He wants to be just like his father.
  (D) He thinks his father should start another business.

Computers

Warm-up

A
Look & Listen

Listen to the dialogs. ((Track 70))

B
Listen Again

Listen again, and match the action with the item. ((Track 71))

1. updating •
2. uploading •
3. downloaded •
4. delete •

• (A) some spam
• (B) a homepage
• (C) some new pictures
• (D) an MP3 file

C
Essential Expressions

Circle the right word.

1. Click "OK" to (choose / upload) the file to the web.
2. Did you (download / type) your password correctly?
3. Every day I have to (delete / search) spam messages from my account.
4. Have you ever (typed / used) a search engine called Metacrawler?
5. There was a problem, so I could not (open / turn on) the webpage.
6. How often do you just (delete / surf) the Internet for fun?
7. Please (copy / use) this email and send it to five friends.
8. The file is big, so it will take several minutes to (download / turn on) the attachment.
9. We can (chat / upload) online about the project this evening.
10. You don't have to do anything to (chat / load) the program. It will do it automatically.

Listening Practice

Listen. Write the answer. ((Track 72))

> It's www.English.co.uk.   You need to download the program's new version.
> Yes, I did.   The server is down.   Yes. The old one didn't work properly.

1. _____
2. _____
3. _____
4. _____
5. _____

B

How would you ask?

Listen. Write the question or statement. ((Track 73))

> What's wrong?   How did you meet him?   How can I get the new version?
> Do you know her email address?   I don't know who sent me this message.

1. _____
2. _____
3. _____
4. _____
5. _____

C

Describe the picture using the words below.

A

Pronunciation Practice

In casual speech, you may hear the word "for" pronounced as "fer."

Written	Spoken
1. Did they buy a new computer for you?	1. Did they buy a new computer fer you?
2. I need to search for the information online.	2. I need to search fer the information online.
3. Let's drop by the computer store for a second.	3. Let's drop by the computer store fer a second.

✓ **Now practice saying the following sentences.**

1. I was online for an hour.
2. The hard drive for that computer is better.
3. What do you use for your password?

✓ **Now listen and repeat.** (((Track **75**)))

B

Conversation Pictures

Listen to the dialogs, and number the pictures. (((Track **76**)))

✓ **Now listen to the dialogs again, and choose the correct activity.**

1. (A) Chat   (B) Email   (C) Play   (D) Surf
2. (A) Chat   (B) Email   (C) Play   (D) Surf
3. (A) Chat   (B) Email   (C) Play   (D) Surf
4. (A) Chat   (B) Email   (C) Play   (D) Surf

Short Dialogs

A

Dialog 1

Listen to the dialog and questions. Choose the best answer. ((Track 77))

1. (A) The hard drive   (B) The keyboard
   (C) The screen   (D) The speakers

2. (A) A laptop   (B) A Mac
   (C) A typewriter   (D) A word processor

✓ **Listen again, and fill in the blanks.**

M: Which computer do you think I should buy?

W: You should get this one. It has more
   ❶_____.

M: But the ❷_____ for that one is so
   big. I kind of like this other one because it
   will take up ❸_____ space.

W: If you're worried about ❹_____,
   maybe you should get one of the new
   ❺_____ instead of a PC.

M: I'm not very familiar with ❻_____.
   I'm more comfortable with a PC.

B

Dialog 2

Listen to the dialog and questions. Choose the best answer. ((Track 78))

1. (A) It has a virus.   (B) It is not finished.
   (C) It is too big.   (D) It is the wrong program.

2. (A) By email   (B) On a CD
   (C) On a disk   (D) Through the network

C

Dialog 3

Listen to the dialog, and number the steps in order from 1-4. ((Track 79))

_____ (A) Click to start

_____ (B) Double-click the icon

_____ (C) Open the folder

_____ (D) Tell it where to save the file

Main Dialog

Listen to the dialog, and choose the best answer. ((Track 80))

1. What did his friend send him?
   - (A) A book
   - (B) An e-card
   - (C) A file
   - (D) A virus

2. What does she think is in the attachment?
   - (A) A computer game
   - (B) A lot of text
   - (C) A virus
   - (D) Songs or speaking

3. What does he need to download?
   - (A) A game
   - (B) A membership form
   - (C) A player
   - (D) A text reader

Listen again, and fill in the blanks. ((Track 81))

M: Could you do me a favor?

W: Sure, what do you need?

M: Do you ❶_____ much about computers?

W: I know a ❷_____.

M: Well, my friend sent me an ❸_____, but I'm having trouble ❹_____ it.

W: Is this the message your friend sent you on the ❺_____ now?

M: Yes, that's it. This is the ❻_____. I downloaded it right here.

W: OK.... It's an "avi" ❼_____. That means your friend sent you a ❽_____ file.

M: Right, he mentioned that in his email. Why can't I ❾_____ it to open?

W: Well, from the looks of it, you probably need to download a ❿_____. I can show you how to do it. It's not that difficult once you know how.

Short Talks

Listen to the short talk and questions. Choose the best answer. ((Track 82))

1. (A) Listening to music   (B) Playing a game
   (C) Protecting computers   (D) Viewing image files

2. (A) Copy itself   (B) Erase itself
   (C) Load itself   (D) Print itself

✓ **Listen again, and fill in the blanks.**

Attention, all network ❶_____. Please visit the following website to download a special patch to ❷_____ all network computers from the Happy ❸_____ worm. Click on the blue ❹_____ for "HB Worm Patch" at www.SecurityPort. ❺_____. The patch will automatically ❻_____ itself when it is downloaded.

Listen to the short talk and questions. Choose the best answer. ((Track 83))

1. (A) Designing websites   (B) Programming computers
   (C) Repairing computers   (D) Using computers

2. (A) Delete buttons   (B) Power buttons
   (C) Save buttons   (D) Tab buttons

Listen to the short talk, and match the information that goes together. ((Track 84))

1. Her family had more than one computer •   • (A) in a bedroom.

2. Her parents' computer was   •   • (B) in the living room.

3. The computer she shared was   •   • (C) in their house.

A

Picture Matching

Listen to the dialogs. Choose the correct picture. ((Track 85))

 **A**

 **B**

 **C**

1. (A)　　　　(B)　　　　(C)

2. (A)　　　　(B)　　　　(C)

B

Listen & Choose

Listen to the dialogs and questions. Choose the best answer. ((Track 86))

3. (A) A virus
   (C) A broken disk
   (B) No power
   (D) No time left

4. (A) He forgot his password.
   (C) The CD player is broken.
   (B) He bought a new computer.
   (D) The program doesn't work.

5. (A) A key word
   (C) An email address
   (B) A search engine
   (D) An Internet server

6. (A) A keyboard
   (C) A monitor
   (B) A memory card
   (D) A mouse

7. (A) It is serious.
   (C) She doesn't believe him.
   (B) It is strange.
   (D) She had a similar problem.

8. (A) Chatting online
   (C) Repairing the computer
   (B) Playing a game
   (D) Writing an essay

9. (A) A Japanese company
   (C) The woman
   (B) The man
   (D) The woman's friend

Wrap-up

Talk about these questions.

1. How old were you when you first used a computer?
2. Did you learn computer skills easily or with difficulty?
3. What is a good age for children to start using computers?

Listen and answer the questions. ((Track 87))

1. **Why do some educators think pre-school children should use computers?**
   Some educators think pre-school children should learn to use computers because
   _____.

2. **Why do some educators think young children should not use computers?**
   Some educators think young children should not use computers because
   _____.

3. **What solution is suggested by the speaker?**
   The speaker suggests that _____.

Listen again, and fill in the blanks. ((Track 88))

At what age ❶_____ a child learn to ❷_____ a computer? The answer ❸_____ to depend on ❹_____ you ask.

Some ❺_____ childhood educators feel ❻_____ "the earlier, the ❼_____." They believe that in ❽_____ society computer skills are a ❾_____ necessity for every ❿_____, just like reading and ⓫_____. Therefore, children should ⓬_____ using and playing with ⓭_____ even while they ⓮_____ in pre-school. Computers ⓯_____ make learning fun and ⓰_____ interactive. For example, a ⓱_____ that teaches reading can ⓲_____ pictures print text, and even ⓳_____ words during a lesson.

However, ⓴_____ educators believe that ㉑_____ could have a negative ㉒_____ on the mental and ㉓_____ development of children. Educators ㉔_____ oppose early computer ㉕_____ by children say that ㉖_____ do not use their imagination ㉗_____. The computer screen ㉘_____ them everything. Also, a ㉙_____ who plays alone on a ㉚_____ does not learn how to ㉛_____ or interact with ㉜_____ children. Physically, children who ㉝_____ for a long time or ㉞_____ a computer mouse too ㉟_____ can develop problems with ㊱_____ parts of their bodies.

㊲_____ the best way for ㊳_____ children to use computers ㊴_____ to use them only ㊵_____ a short time each ㊶_____. If a child uses a ㊷_____ for thirty minutes each ㊸_____, she or he still has ㊹_____ of time to learn and ㊺_____ away from the computer.

Listening Test

PART I: Picture Description (((Track 89)))

Listen and choose the statement that best describes what you see in the picture.

1.

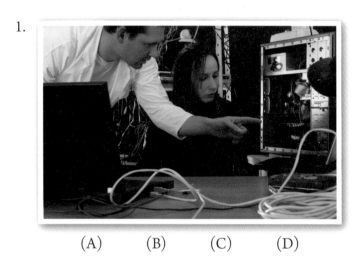

    (A)   (B)   (C)   (D)

2.

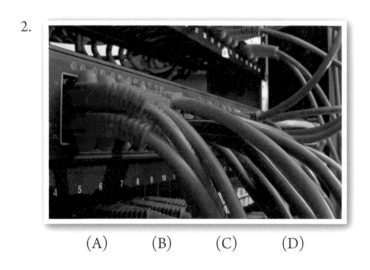

    (A)   (B)   (C)   (D)

3.

    (A)   (B)   (C)   (D)

4.

(A)   (B)   (C)   (D)

5.

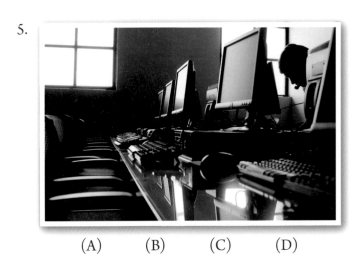

(A)   (B)   (C)   (D)

PART II: Questions and Responses ((Track 90))

Listen and choose the best response to each question.

6. (A)   (B)   (C)

7. (A)   (B)   (C)

8. (A)   (B)   (C)

9. (A)   (B)   (C)

10. (A)   (B)   (C)

PART III: Short Conversations ((Track 91))

You will hear two dialogs, each followed by three questions. Listen carefully, and choose the best answer to each question.

11. What are the speakers talking about?

   (A) Old computers
   (B) An office friend
   (C) A storage disc
   (D) An updated software program

12. What did the woman say about the cost?

   (A) It was inexpensive.
   (B) It was too expensive.
   (C) It was a reasonable price.
   (D) It was more expensive than the older version.

13. What did the man think of the older version?

   (A) He didn't like it.
   (B) He thought it was difficult to learn.
   (C) He thought it was easier to use.
   (D) He wanted to get a tutorial.

---

14. What did the woman open?

   (A) A folder with saved files
   (B) A virus scanner
   (C) A webpage with images
   (D) Her email account

15. What did the man want the woman to edit?

   (A) The document file
   (B) The text file and the original file
   (C) Only the text file
   (D) None of the above

16. What is the woman's job?

   (A) A newscaster
   (B) A computer technician
   (C) A movie director
   (D) An editor

PART IV: Short Talks ((Track 92))

You will hear two talks, each followed by three questions. Listen carefully, and choose the best answer to each question.

17. What is *Tech Pro*?

(A) A language tutor
(B) An online game
(C) A photo editor
(D) A word processor

18. What is the speaker's opinion of *Tech Pro*?

(A) It's boring.
(B) It's cheap.
(C) It's great.
(D) It's terrible.

19. How long is the tutorial?

(A) A few minutes
(B) About an hour
(C) Almost thirty slides
(D) Not mentioned

---

20. What does the mouse include?

(A) Memory chips
(B) Extra large buttons
(C) A sensitive ball
(D) A laser

21. Which surface could this mouse work on?

(A) A plastic counter
(B) A glass tabletop
(C) A piece of paper
(D) All of the above

22. Which of the following is true?

(A) This mouse is very expensive.
(B) This mouse is the latest design.
(C) There are advantages to using an optical mouse.
(D) Mouses work better on plastic counters.

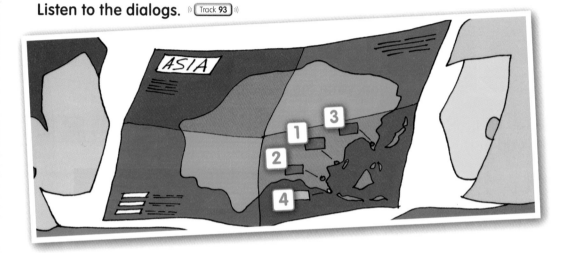

5 Travel

Warm-up

A
Look & Listen

Listen to the dialogs. ((Track 93))

B
Listen Again

Listen again, and fill in the blanks. ((Track 94))

1. She enjoyed _____ in _____.
2. He went to a great _____ in _____.
3. She remembers the wonderful _____ in _____.
4. He has good memories of the _____ in _____.

C
Essential Expressions

Write the missing phrases to make correct sentences.

beautiful postcard	carry-on luggage	expensive resort	heavy traffic
historic statue	big fountain	royal palace	scenic harbor
	street market	tropical island	

1. All of your meals are included in the fee for your stay, so it's a(n) _____.
2. Thank you for mailing me that _____.
3. I hope my _____ is not too big or too heavy to take on the plane.
4. The _____ that we saw in the park looked like a king or a general.
5. We enjoyed watching the sailboats going in and out of the _____.
6. It will be faster to take the subway due to the _____ on the streets right now.
7. The last king who lived in the _____ died about fifty years ago.
8. We saw some children playing in the water in the _____.
9. You can buy lots of delicious food and nice souvenirs at the _____.
10. The only way to get to the _____ is by boat since there is no airport on it.

Listening Practice

A

How would you answer?

Listen. Write the answer. ((Track 95))

> It rained quite a bit.   My sister.   Six hours.
> No, the price was very reasonable.   Yes, we had a great time.

1. _____
2. _____
3. _____
4. _____
5. _____

B

How would you ask?

Listen. Write the question. ((Track 96))

> Did you rent a car?   How many days were you there?
> Was the beach nice?   How was it?   Where did you go?

1. _____
2. _____
3. _____
4. _____
5. _____

C

Picture Description

Describe the picture using the words below.

| airplane | electronic | sleep | expression |

_____

_____

_____

_____

✓ **Listen to the description of the picture.** ((Track 97))

Speaking Practice

In casual speech, you may hear the word "you" pronounced as "ja" or the words "your" pronounced as "jer" after words that end with -d.

Written	Spoken
1. Did you spend much time in Rome?	1. Did ja spend much time in Rome?
2. I heard you went to Hawaii.	2. I heard ja went to Hawaii.
3. What did you think of Istanbul?	3. What did ja think of Istanbul?

✓ **Now practice saying the following sentences.**

1. What surprised you the most about Brazil?
2. Where did you take this picture?
3. Did you spend your whole vacation there?

✓ **Now listen and repeat.** ((Track 98))

Listen to the dialogs, and number the pictures. ((Track 99))

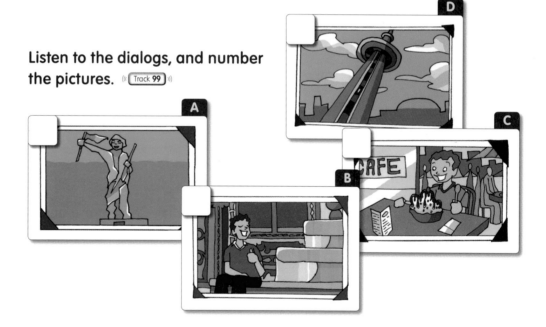

✓ **Now listen to the dialogs again, and choose the correct location.**

1. (A) Palace   (B) Market   (C) Museum   (D) Restaurant
2. (A) Palace   (B) Market   (C) Museum   (D) Restaurant
3. (A) Palace   (B) Market   (C) Museum   (D) Restaurant
4. (A) Palace   (B) Market   (C) Museum   (D) Restaurant

Short Dialogs

Dialog 1

Listen to the dialog and questions. Choose the best answer. ((Track 100))

1. (A) Two weeks   (B) A month
   (C) Five weeks   (D) One year

2. (A) Learn Spanish   (B) See special sights
   (C) Take pictures   (D) Teach English

✓ **Listen again, and fill in the blanks.**

W: Do you have any plans for your ❶_____ vacation?

M: Didn't I tell you? I'm going to ❷_____!

W: No, you didn't ❸_____ me. When are you leaving?

M: I leave on ❹_____ 4th. I don't come back until ❺_____ 12th.

W: Are you just going to be traveling around the country all that time?

M: No, I'm going to be ❻_____ Spanish in Guanajuato.

Dialog 2

Listen to the dialog and questions. Choose the best answer. ((Track 101))

1. (A) A CD of pop music   (B) A picture of a famous place
   (C) A small statue   (D) Something to eat

2. (A) April   (B) July
   (C) October   (D) January

Dialog 3

Listen to the dialog, and complete each statement. ((Track 102))

1. It is not a good day to visit the _____.

2. They can take pictures near a _____ in front of the _____.

Listen

Listen to the dialog, and choose the best answer. ((Track 103))

1. During which season was their vacation?
   - (A) Spring
   - (B) Summer
   - (C) Fall
   - (D) Winter

2. What has she heard about in Colorado?
   - (A) Its animals
   - (B) Its mountains
   - (C) Its weather
   - (D) Its vacation spots

3. Which is true about the woman?
   - (A) She doesn't like cold weather.
   - (B) She doesn't like to travel.
   - (C) She has relatives in Miami.
   - (D) She isn't good at sports.

Listen Again

Listen again, and fill in the blanks. ((Track 104))

W: Hey! It's great to see you again! How was your ❶_____ vacation?

M: It was great! I had so much fun!

W: So . . . where did you go?

M: Oh, on my winter vacation? I went ❷_____ in Colorado.

W: How ❸_____ it? I heard there are some really nice ❹_____ in Colorado.

M: Fantastic! I had a ❺_____ time. We went to this ❻_____ called Copper Creek. If you ever get a chance to go there, I ❼_____ recommend it.

W: Well . . . I don't know. I don't really like skiing or ❽_____. Cold weather really bothers me.

M: Oh? Well you look really rested. Where did you spend your ❾_____ vacation?

W: On a ❿_____ in Miami.

Short Talks

A
Short Talk 1

Listen to the short talk and questions. Choose the best answer. (((Track 105)))

1. (A) They are less strict than in the past.
   (B) They are followed around the world.
   (C) They are stricter than in the past.
   (D) They are the same as in the past.

2. (A) Their bags   (B) Their children
   (C) Their flights   (D) Their tickets

✓ **Listen again, and fill in the blanks.**

❶_____ to the Phoenix International Airport.
Due to ❷_____ security measures, airport
security ❸_____ all passengers to carefully
watch their ❹_____. Do not leave your luggage
unattended. Also, do not ❺_____ or accept any
❻_____ from strangers. Thank you.

B
Short Talk 2

Listen to the short talk and questions. Choose the best answer. (((Track 106)))

1. (A) His girlfriend   (B) His parents
   (C) His roommate   (D) His sister

2. (A) By car   (B) On foot
   (C) By plane   (D) By train

C
Short Talk 3

Listen to the short talk, and circle the activities that the speaker mentions. (((Track 107)))

going to the beach

packing her luggage

seeing the palace

shopping at the street market

visiting the spa

waiting in traffic

Listening Quiz

03:55

A

Picture Matching

Listen to the dialogs. Choose the correct picture. ((Track 108))

 **A**

 **B**

 **C**

1. (A) (B) (C)

2. (A) (B) (C)

B

Listen & Choose

Listen to the dialogs and questions. Choose the best answer. ((Track 109))

3. (A) England
   (C) Germany
   (B) France
   (D) Switzerland

4. (A) Their color
   (C) Their location
   (B) Their history
   (D) Their size

5. (A) The man
   (C) The woman's mother
   (B) The woman
   (D) The woman and her mother

6. (A) By car
   (C) By ship
   (B) By plane
   (D) By train

7. (A) He didn't like it.
   (C) He was pleased.
   (B) He enjoyed it.
   (D) He was terrified.

8. (A) In a boat
   (C) In a plane
   (B) In a car
   (D) On a horse

9. (A) Bad directions
   (C) Bad traffic
   (B) Bad food
   (D) Bad weather

Wrap-up

A

Pre-listening Discussion

Talk about these questions.

1. Which countries in Africa are famous for travelers?
2. What kinds of animals can people see on safaris?
3. How much would you expect to pay for a safari? (per day)

B

Listening Comprehension

Listen and answer the questions. ((Track 110))

1. **Which country is most famous for its safari tours?**
   The country that is most famous for safaris is _____.

2. **What are the "big five"?**
   The "big five" are _____
   _____.

3. **How much might a "cheap" three-day safari cost?**
   A "cheap" three-day safari might cost _____.

C

Dictation Practice

Listen again, and fill in the blanks. ((Track 111))

Are you interested in ❶_____ how animals live in the ❷_____? Have you ever thought ❸_____ taking an African safari? ❹_____ you think you might ❺_____ to go on one ❻_____, here are some tips to ❼_____ in mind.

The most ❽_____ country in Africa for ❾_____ travelers is Kenya. Kenya has many ❿_____ national animal reserves. The ⓫_____ also has the ⓬_____ developed safari industry as ⓭_____ as tourism is concerned. ⓮_____ travelers can see all ⓯_____ the "big five" safari ⓰_____ in Kenya: lions, buffalos, ⓱_____, rhinos, and leopards. Of ⓲_____, Kenya isn't the only ⓳_____ for safari travelers. Other ⓴_____ well known in Africa ㉑_____ safari tourism are Tanzania, ㉒_____ Africa, and Swaziland.

When ㉓_____ a safari, travelers should ㉔_____ to pay over $1,000 ㉕_____ person for the trip. ㉖_____ companies in Africa offer ㉗_____ different packages, so prices ㉘_____ vary a lot. For ㉙_____ who don't mind ㉚_____ on the ground ㉛_____ eating camp food, safaris ㉜_____ cost about $100 per ㉝_____. On the other hand, ㉞_____ can pay $500 per ㉟_____ or more to sleep in ㊱_____ hotels each night while on ㊲_____ and eat better food. The ㊳_____ idea for travelers is to ㊴_____ a safari through a travel ㊵_____ who specializes in safari ㊶_____. They will know the ㊷_____ companies and will get the ㊸_____ prices.

Listening Test 🕐 08:24

PART I: Picture Description ((Track 112))

Listen and choose the statement that best describes what you see in the picture.

1.

(A)   (B)   (C)   (D)

2.

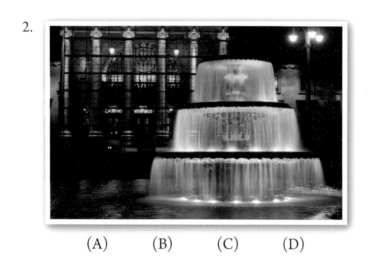

(A)   (B)   (C)   (D)

3.

(A)   (B)   (C)   (D)

4.

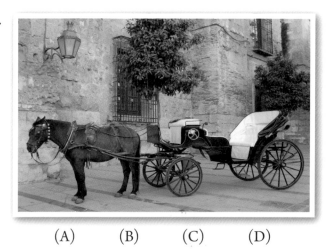

(A)   (B)   (C)   (D)

5.

(A)   (B)   (C)   (D)

PART II: Questions and Responses ((Track 113))

Listen and choose the best response to each question.

6. (A)   (B)   (C)

7. (A)   (B)   (C)

8. (A)   (B)   (C)

9. (A)   (B)   (C)

10. (A)   (B)   (C)

PART III: Short Conversations (((Track 114)))

You will hear two dialogs, each followed by three questions. Listen carefully, and choose the best answer to each question.

11. What does the man recommend?

    (A) Driving along the shore

    (B) Eating downtown

    (C) Going out of the city

    (D) Visiting a museum

12. What does the first speaker plan to do?

    (A) Cross the English Channel

    (B) Take a train

    (C) Rent a car

    (D) Visit an old castle

13. What difficulty did the man predict?

    (A) Understanding the language

    (B) Driving on the other side of the road

    (C) Adjusting to the food

    (D) Wearing warm clothes

---

14. What will they do on their last day?

    (A) Go hiking

    (B) Go shopping

    (C) Go sightseeing

    (D) Go and see a cultural performance

15. What might change their plans for tomorrow?

    (A) They have to change their departure date.

    (B) It will be a holiday.

    (C) It might rain tomorrow.

    (D) They have to check out early from the hotel.

16. What does one of the speakers need to do tomorrow?

    (A) Buy some souvenirs

    (B) Make a reservation

    (C) Call the airport

    (D) Wear warm clothing

PART IV: Short Talks ((Track 115))

You will hear two talks, each followed by three questions. Listen carefully, and choose the best answer to each question.

17. What is the speaker doing?
    - (A) Describing a picture
    - (B) Offering tour options to a client
    - (C) Reading a travel guide
    - (D) Visiting a tourist attraction

18. Which of the following is true?
    - (A) Pictures were not allowed.
    - (B) The cathedral was closed for the day.
    - (C) The speaker did not join a tour.
    - (D) The speaker worked as a tour guide.

19. What was inside this place?
    - (A) Performers
    - (B) Plants
    - (C) Sculptures
    - (D) Shops

---

20. Where might you hear this announcement?
    - (A) At an airport
    - (B) At a bus station
    - (C) At a ferry port
    - (D) At a train station

21. Where should passengers go?
    - (A) Baggage claim
    - (B) Pier Two
    - (C) Platform D
    - (D) The ticket counter

22. What did the announcer NOT tell the passengers?
    - (A) Passengers must go through customs.
    - (B) Tickets will be verified.
    - (C) The ferry will leave when all passengers are on board.
    - (D) The ferry is ready to be boarded.

Restaurants

Warm-up

Listen to the dialogs. (((Track 116)))

Listen again, and match the person with the phrase. (((Track 117)))

	Server	Customer
1. Sure. Spaghetti and extra garlic bread.	☐	☐
2. . . . with the sauce on the side?	☐	☐
3. The hot wings come in two sizes . . .	☐	☐
4. Would you like strawberry or blueberry topping . . . ?	☐	☐

Match the right response for each question.

1. What kind of atmosphere did the restaurant have? •
2. Could I get a refill for my coffee, please? •
3. What kind of dressing would you like on your salad? •
4. Do you want to pick up some Chinese food? •
5. Would you like any topping on your ice cream? •
6. What would you like on the side? •
7. How many people are in your party, ma'am? •
8. When will a table for four be available? •
9. Why didn't you like the restaurant? •
10. Would you like to share a dessert with me? •

- (A) I'll bring that right out, sir.
- (B) No, let's get it delivered.
- (C) I'll have the vegetable of the day.
- (D) The service was terrible there.
- (E) Sure. Let's split a piece of cake.
- (F) I'll take Italian on the side, please.
- (G) There are eight of us.
- (H) It was a casual place.
- (I) No, thanks. Plain is fine.
- (J) In about fifteen minutes.

Listening Practice

Listen. Write the answer. ((Track 118))

I'll bring more right away.	Medium well, please.
No, I think that's it.	Right over there.	Yes, we are.

1. _____
2. _____
3. _____
4. _____
5. _____

Listen. Write the question. ((Track 119))

Can I take that plate for you?	How many are in your party?
Coffee or dessert? Is this table alright?	What would you like to drink?

1. _____
2. _____
3. _____
4. _____
5. _____

Describe the picture using the words below.

chef	wok	fry	ladle

✓ **Listen to the description of the picture.** ((Track 120))

Speaking Practice

A

Intonation Practice

In certain three-syllable statements or questions, the stress should be on the second syllable. Say the following statements and questions using the stress pattern "dum da dum."

Written	Spoken
1. A hot dog.	1. A **hot** dog.
2. Let's try it.	2. Let's **try** it.
3. Potato	3. Po**ta**to

✓ **Now practice saying the following sentences. Remember to stress the second syllable.**

1. Let's get some.
2. For you, sir?
3. How is it?

✓ **Now listen and repeat.** ((Track 121))

B

Conversation Pictures

Listen to the dialogs, and number the pictures. ((Track 122))

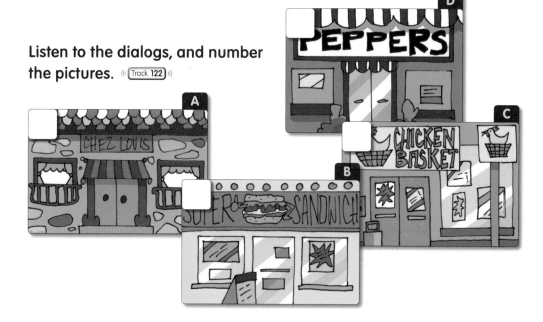

✓ **Now listen to the dialogs again, and choose what is described for each place.**

1. (A) Atmosphere   (B) Price   (C) Service   (D) Size
2. (A) Atmosphere   (B) Price   (C) Service   (D) Size
3. (A) Atmosphere   (B) Price   (C) Service   (D) Size
4. (A) Atmosphere   (B) Price   (C) Service   (D) Size

Short Dialogs

 A

Dialog 1

Listen to the dialog and questions. Choose the best answer. ((Track 123))

1. (A) They are vegetarians.
   (B) They have not eaten all day.
   (C) They finished dinner.
   (D) They like expensive food.

2. (A) A hot drink
   (B) Cooked vegetables
   (C) Fried cheese
   (D) Something sweet

✓ **Listen again, and fill in the blanks.**

M: I am so ❶_____!

W: Me, too. That ❷_____ delicious.

M: How about splitting ❸_____?

W: What were you ❹_____ to order?

M: The fried ❺_____.

W: I might just have one ❻_____.

B

Dialog 2

Listen to the dialog and questions. Choose the best answer. ((Track 124))

1. (A) At a table in a restaurant
   (B) At a restaurant's bar
   (C) At a restaurant's entrance
   (D) In a restaurant's kitchen

2. (A) A table is ready.
   (B) He has to wait.
   (C) He needs a reservation.
   (D) The restaurant is closed.

C

Dialog 3

Listen to the dialog and questions. Complete the answers. ((Track 125))

1. She will eat leftover _____.
2. It was delivered _____.

Main Dialog

Listen

Listen to the dialog, and choose the best answer. ((Track 126))

1. What does the woman do?
   - (A) Give him the bill
   - (B) Move him to another table
   - (C) Take him to the table
   - (D) Take his order

2. What does the man want to drink?
   - (A) Cola
   - (B) Tea
   - (C) Water
   - (D) Nothing

3. What does the man want to eat?
   - (A) A potato and salad
   - (B) A sandwich and French fries
   - (C) A sandwich and salad
   - (D) Steak and a potato

Listen Again

Listen again, and fill in the blanks. ((Track 127))

W: Welcome. How are you this ❶_____?

M: I'm great, thanks.

W: My name is Jennifer and I'll be ❷_____ you today. I'll give you a couple of minutes to take a look at our appetizers. While you're taking a look, can I take your ❸_____ order to start off?

M: Nothing special, thanks. I'll just have ❹_____.

W: OK. Have you had a chance to look at our ❺_____?

M: I come here all the time, so I already ❻_____ what I'd like to order.

W: Alright. What would you like ❼_____?

M: I'll have the ❽_____ sandwich with a green salad on the side instead of French fries.

W: A turkey ❾_____ with a side salad. I'll bring that ❿_____ out for you.

Short Talks

A

Short Talk 1

Listen to the short talk and questions. Choose the best answer. ((Track 128))

1. (A) Beef   (B) Chicken
   (C) Fish   (D) Pork

2. (A) Beans   (B) Chicken
   (C) Onions   (D) Tomatoes

✓ **Listen again, and fill in the blanks.**

Good ❶_____, and welcome to Henderson's.
My name is Chris and I'll be your ❷_____ this
evening. Our special tonight is grilled ❸_____
with Italian vegetables. And the ❹_____ of the
day is ❺_____ soup. What would you
❻_____ to drink this evening?

B

Short Talk 2

Listen to the short talk and questions. Choose the best answer. ((Track 129))

1. (A) Fifteen minutes   (B) Half an hour
   (C) Forty minutes   (D) One and a half hours

2. (A) Go to the store   (B) Order a pizza
   (C) Call the store   (D) Visit a website

C

Short Talk 3

Listen to the short talk, and write T for true or F for false for each statement. ((Track 130))

1. _____ The speaker works at a small café.
2. _____ None of the people working at the café know him.
3. _____ The café serves sandwiches.

Listening Quiz

03:31

A
Picture Matching

Listen to the dialogs. Choose the correct picture. ((Track 131))

 A

 B

 C

1. (A)   (B)   (C)

2. (A)   (B)   (C)

B
Listen & Choose

Listen to the dialogs and questions. Choose the best answer. ((Track 132))

3. (A) A salad   (B) A hamburger
   (C) Grilled fish   (D) The special

4. (A) A drink   (B) A sandwich
   (C) Soup   (D) The server

5. (A) Just salad   (B) Just soup
   (C) Steak and salad   (D) Soup and a sandwich

6. (A) She ate a lot.   (B) She didn't bring a spoon.
   (C) She is hungry.   (D) She doesn't have much money.

7. (A) Asking for a menu   (B) Checking the price
   (C) Ordering food   (D) Reserving a table

8. (A) Items on the menu   (B) Places to eat
   (C) Staff at the restaurant   (D) The food they will cook

9. (A) Cheese pizza   (B) Fried chicken
   (C) Grilled salmon   (D) Rice and tofu

Wrap-up

Talk about these questions.

1. How many meals did you eat yesterday?
2. How many snacks did you eat?
3. Was that a typical day for your eating habits?

Listen and answer the questions. ((Track 133))

1. **How are people's eating habits different today compared to the past?**
   People's eating habits today are different because they _____
   _____ .

2. **How many times each day does the average person eat?**
   The average person eats _____ times each day.

3. **What kinds of technology have affected society's eating habits?**
   _____ and _____ have affected society's eating habits.

Listen again, and fill in the blanks. ((Track 134))

    People's eating habits are ❶_____. In the past, people ❷_____ three
meals a day. But ❸_____, the fast pace of ❹_____ in modern society does
❺_____ leave enough time for ❻_____ people to make or ❼_____ three
full meals. A ❽_____ showed that one out of ❾_____ people only has time
to ❿_____ two or fewer square ⓫_____ a day. Instead, people who skip meals
⓬_____ eating snacks. In fact, the ⓭_____ person eats four times ⓮_____
the day, including meals ⓯_____ snacks. That is just the ⓰_____ person,
though. Some people ⓱_____ they eat six times ⓲_____ day!
    It is not ⓳_____ longer hours of work ⓴_____ have affected modern
eating ㉑_____. Modern technology has also ㉒_____ the way people eat
㉓_____. For example, look at ㉔_____ cars have affected eating ㉕_____.
First, cars became popular, ㉖_____ then fast food was ㉗_____ so that people
could ㉘_____ in their cars. ㉙_____, many fast food chains ㉚_____
trying to create more ㉛_____ of foods that are ㉜_____ for drivers to eat
㉝_____ on the road.
    Computers ㉞_____ also changed modern eating ㉟_____. Teenagers
don't want to ㊱_____ time away from surfing the Internet ㊲_____ gaming, so they
snack ㊳_____ front of their computers. ㊴_____, with so many people
㊵_____ to computers in the ㊶_____, at home, and on the ㊷_____,
it is becoming less ㊸_____ less common for people to ㊹_____ a relaxed meal
with ㊺_____ or friends.

PART I: Picture Description (((Track 135)))

Listen and choose the statement that best describes what you see in the picture.

1.

   (A)   (B)   (C)   (D)

2.

   (A)   (B)   (C)   (D)

3.

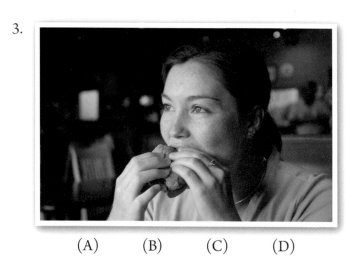

   (A)   (B)   (C)   (D)

4.

(A)   (B)   (C)   (D)

5.

(A)   (B)   (C)   (D)

PART II: Questions and Responses ((Track 136))

Listen and choose the best response to each question.

6. (A)   (B)   (C)

7. (A)   (B)   (C)

8. (A)   (B)   (C)

9. (A)   (B)   (C)

10. (A)   (B)   (C)

PART III: Short Conversations ((Track 137))

You will hear two dialogs, each followed by three questions. Listen carefully, and choose the best answer to each question.

11. Where are the speakers?

   (A) In a restaurant
   (B) At a picnic
   (C) At an outdoor barbecue
   (D) At a dinner party

12. Who are the speakers?

   (A) A cook and a waitress
   (B) A couple eating dinner together
   (C) A manager and an employee
   (D) A server and a customer

13. Why did the customer need more time?

   (A) She didn't understand the menu.
   (B) They didn't have the dish she wanted.
   (C) She was waiting for her friends to order.
   (D) She is a picky eater.

---

14. Which of the following is probably true?

   (A) They are vegetarians.
   (B) They have never been to this restaurant.
   (C) They have not ordered yet.
   (D) They just finished the main course.

15. What does the woman want to do?

   (A) Change the subject
   (B) Order the main dish
   (C) Eat healthier foods
   (D) Order the chicken wings

16. What did the man want to do?

   (A) Order many different kinds of foods
   (B) Share an order
   (C) Have some dessert
   (D) Change their table

PART IV: Short Talks ((Track 138))

You will hear two talks, each followed by three questions. Listen carefully, and choose the best answer to each question.

17. What is new about Dixie Chicken?

    (A) A new restaurant has opened.
    (B) The hours of the restaurant have changed.
    (C) The parking lot has expanded.
    (D) They have added items to the menu.

18. What kind of food does Dixie Chicken serve?

    (A) Burgers and sandwiches
    (B) Chicken curry
    (C) Chicken wings and snacks
    (D) Fried chicken

19. Where is Dixie Chicken's original location?

    (A) At the mall
    (B) On North Shore Avenue
    (C) Next to Maxwell's
    (D) Downtown

---

20. What might be a problem?

    (A) The food is not good.
    (B) The location is inconvenient.
    (C) The room is too small.
    (D) The schedule is too strict.

21. What will the caller do?

    (A) Call again later
    (B) Check the restaurant website
    (C) Visit the restaurant tomorrow
    (D) Wait for a return call

22. What did the caller want?

    (A) A better room
    (B) More information
    (C) To move the party to a different restaurant
    (D) To talk to the manager

Hotels

Warm-up

Listen to the dialogs. ((Track 139))

Listen again, and fill in the blanks. ((Track 140))

1. Mr. Johnson will stay for _____.
2. They will meet a man named _____ in the _____.
3. The woman wants to get some _____ from the _____.
4. The man will get his _____ from the _____.

Circle the best word or phrase to complete each question.

1. Are all of the rooms in the hotel (first floor / non-smoking rooms)?
2. What do you want to buy from the (gift shop / sauna)?
3. Can you help me fill out this (registration form / room rate)?
4. Do you want to wait for me in the (air conditioner / lobby)?
5. What time should we ask for a (room key / wake-up call)?
6. Does the room have (a double bed / an elevator) in it?
7. Which floor is the (airport shuttle / indoor pool) on?
8. Is there anyone working at the (front desk / ice machine)?
9. Would you like to order (maid service / room service) for breakfast?
10. What time should we (check out / check in) on the day we leave the hotel?

Listening Practice

Listen. Write the answer. ((Track 141))

> Sixty-five dollars. Yes, it does. The Oceanside Resort.
> The third floor. Yes, we had a wonderful time.

1. _____
2. _____
3. _____
4. _____
5. _____

Listen. Write the question. ((Track 142))

> Can we get some extra towels? Does the gift shop sell toothpaste?
> How far is it from the hotel? Should we meet in the lobby?
> What time is check-out?

1. _____
2. _____
3. _____
4. _____
5. _____

Describe the picture using the words below.

> receptionist front desk handed beside

✓ **Listen to the description of the picture.** ((Track 143))

Speaking Practice

A

Pronunciation Practice

In casual speech, you may hear the phrase "want to" pronounced as "wanna."

Written	Spoken
1. Do you want to wait in the lobby?	1. Do you wanna wait in the lobby?
2. I want to drop by the gift shop.	2. I wanna drop by the gift shop.
3. Which hotel do you want to stay at?	3. Which hotel do you wanna stay at?

✓ **Now practice saying the following sentences.**

1. I want to turn on the air conditioner.
2. If you want to make a reservation, I can help you with that.
3. Why do you want to get up so early?

✓ **Now listen and repeat.** ((Track 144))

B

Conversation Pictures

Listen to the dialogs, and number the pictures. ((Track 145))

✓ **Now listen to the dialogs again, and choose the correct time of each activity.**

1. (A) Five   (B) Now   (C) Six   (D) Any time
2. (A) Five   (B) Now   (C) Six   (D) Any time
3. (A) Five   (B) Now   (C) Six   (D) Any time
4. (A) Five   (B) Now   (C) Six   (D) Any time

Short Dialogs

Listen to the dialog and questions. Choose the best answer. ((Track 146))

1. (A) Checking in (B) Checking out
   (C) Ordering food (D) Reserving a room

2. (A) It is available any time. (B) It is served in the room.
   (C) It is free. (D) The price will be added to her bill.

✓ **Listen again, and fill in the blanks.**

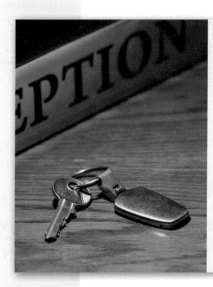

M: Here is your key, ma'am. I hope you enjoy your
   ❶_____.

W: Thank you. I'm sure I will. Oh, I have one
   ❷_____ for you. Do you serve a
   complimentary breakfast in the ❸_____?

M: Yes, ma'am, we do. A continental breakfast is served
   here in the ❹_____ lounge.

W: What time do you start ❺_____ breakfast?

M: Breakfast is available from ❻_____ until nine.

Listen to the dialog and questions. Choose the best answer. ((Track 147))

1. (A) A conference (B) A reunion
   (C) A wedding (D) A sporting event

2. (A) Before ten (B) After midnight
   (C) Around dawn (D) At noon

Listen to the dialog, and choose the right word to complete each sentence. ((Track 148))

1. They will stay at a hotel near (downtown / the airport).

2. They will use a rental car to go (downtown / to the airport).

Main Dialog

Listen to the dialog, and choose the best answer. ((Track 149))

1. When does the man need the room?
   - (A) For last night
   - (B) For this night
   - (C) For tomorrow night
   - (D) For next week

2. How many people will be sharing the room with the man?
   - (A) None
   - (B) One
   - (C) Two
   - (D) Three

3. What is special about the man's room?
   - (A) It has a refrigerator.
   - (B) It has air conditioning.
   - (C) It is on the first floor.
   - (D) It is a non-smoking room.

Listen again, and fill in the blanks. ((Track 150))

W: Good ❶_____, sir. How can I help you this evening?

M: Hi. Do you have any rooms available for ❷_____?

W: Yes, we do. Will you need a room for just ❸_____?

M: No. My wife and our ❹_____ children are outside waiting in the car.

W: I see. Well, I'll check this very quickly for you. We do have a few rooms available with two ❺_____ beds.

M: That will be fine. How much is it ❻_____ to be per night?

W: Well, the basic rate is ❼_____ per night.

M: Oh, and I almost forgot. That's a ❽_____ room, isn't it?

W: Yes, sir. It is. If you'd like to ❾_____ the room, I will need you to fill out this registration ❿_____.

Check

HOTE

FRONT DES

Short Talks

Listen to the short talk and questions. Choose the best answer. ((Track 151))

1. (A) A single room
   (C) A standard suite
   (B) A double room
   (D) A luxury suite

2. (A) Buffet
   (C) French
   (B) Chinese
   (D) Italian

✓ **Listen again, and fill in the blanks.**

It's not too late to make ❶_____ for New Year's Eve! North Park Hotel is now offering a special New Year's ❷_____. For the low price of just ❸_____, you will receive two tickets to the New Year's Ball in North Park Tower, a ❹_____ suite for one night, and complimentary ❺_____ at North Park's five-star ❻_____ restaurant. Call now and make this a New Year's to remember.

Listen to the short talk and questions. Choose the best answer. ((Track 152))

1. (A) A single hotel
   (C) A country
   (B) A city
   (D) Anywhere in the world

2. (A) Cancel a reservation
   (C) Check a reservation
   (B) Change a reservation
   (D) Pay for a reservation

Listen to the short talk. Check (✓) the things the speaker wanted. ((Track 153))

- [ ] Non-smoking room
- [ ] Smoking room
- [ ] Double bed
- [ ] Two single beds
- [ ] One night
- [ ] Two nights

Listening Quiz

03:54

A

Picture Matching

Listen to the dialogs. Choose the correct picture. (((Track 154)))

A

B

C

1. (A)   (B)   (C)

2. (A)   (B)   (C)

B

Listen & Choose

Listen to the dialogs and questions. Choose the best answer. (((Track 155)))

3. (A) A drink   (B) Ice
   (C) A bucket   (D) A drink and ice

4. (A) It was dirty.   (B) It was on an upper floor.
   (C) It was too expensive.   (D) It was too small.

5. (A) A telephone   (B) Clothes hangers
   (C) Room service   (D) Towels

6. (A) She found the pool.   (B) She is hungry.
   (C) She lost something.   (D) She needs a new key.

7. (A) Call another number   (B) Come down to the desk
   (C) Have a nice day   (D) Pay extra money

8. (A) Open the window   (B) Reserve the room
   (C) Sit in the hot sun   (D) Turn on the air conditioner

9. (A) Open the window   (B) Reserve the room
   (C) Sit in the hot sun   (D) Turn on the air conditioner

Wrap-up

A Pre-listening Discussion

Talk about these questions.

1. What is the best hotel you have stayed in?
2. What did you like about this hotel?
3. Which do you prefer, large hotels or small hotels? Why?

B Listening Comprehension

Listen and answer the questions. Track 156

1. **How is a room in a B&B different from a room in other hotels?**
   A room in a B&B is different from a room in other hotels because ____________
   ____.
2. **Where might a B&B hold a "social hour?"**
   A B&B might hold a "social hour" ______________________________.
3. **How is breakfast at a B&B different from breakfast at other hotels?**
   Breakfast at a B&B is different from breakfast at other hotels because __________
   ____.

C Dictation Practice

Listen again, and fill in the blanks. Track 157

As any well-traveled ❶________ can tell you, hotels ❷________ in all shapes and ❸________. Depending on a person's ❹________, travelers can find a ❺________ range of accommodations ❻________ huge resorts and ❼________ to small roadside ❽________. However, there are ❾________ special types of ❿________ that are run by people from ⓫________ own homes. These are ⓬________ Bed and Breakfast Inns, ⓭_____ simply shortened to ⓮________. Often considered to be ⓯________ welcoming than larger ⓰______ chains, B&Bs can ⓱________ a welcome change for ⓲________ or business travelers from ⓳________ types of hotels.

At a ⓴________, the guest sleeps in ㉑________ of the rooms of the ㉒________. Usually these rooms are furnished ㉓________ antique furniture. Sometimes ㉔________ contain something that ㉕_____ unique for their ㉖________. As a ㉗________ in the house, people are ㉘________ to make themselves at ㉙________ in other rooms of the ㉚________, including the living room, ㉛________, porch, or kitchen. In ㉜________, many B&Bs schedule "social ㉝________" in the evening in the ㉞________ or dining room. At ㉟________ times, guests can meet ㊱________ people staying at the ㊲________ or chat with the ㊳________.

Another nice thing about ㊴________ inns is that breakfast ㊵________ with the room, as ㊶________ might guess from the ㊷________ Bed and Breakfast. However, ㊸________________ at a B&B is ㊹________ just cold donuts, toast, and ㊺________ like many hotels serve ㊻_____ the morning. The owner ㊼_____ the B&B typically prepares a ㊽________________ meal for guests.

PART I: Picture Description ((Track 158))

Listen and choose the statement that best describes what you see in the picture.

1.

   (A)   (B)   (C)   (D)

2.

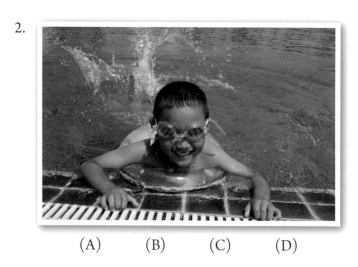

   (A)   (B)   (C)   (D)

3.

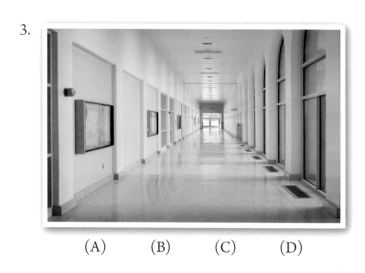

   (A)   (B)   (C)   (D)

4.

(A)   (B)   (C)   (D)

5.

(A)   (B)   (C)   (D)

PART II: Questions and Responses ((Track 159))

Listen and choose the best response to each question.

6. (A)   (B)   (C)

7. (A)   (B)   (C)

8. (A)   (B)   (C)

9. (A)   (B)   (C)

10. (A)   (B)   (C)

PART III: Short Conversations ((Track 160))

You will hear two dialogs, each followed by three questions. Listen carefully, and choose the best answer to each question.

11. Where is the speaker?
    - (A) In a hotel room
    - (B) In a travel agency
    - (C) At a restaurant
    - (D) In a garage

12. What is the man doing?
    - (A) Asking for directions
    - (B) Making a reservation
    - (C) Ordering food
    - (D) Requesting a wake-up call

13. What was the speaker's response to the request?
    - (A) It will be brought up immediately.
    - (B) They do not have that order.
    - (C) It will take an hour to be delivered.
    - (D) It will take about fifteen minutes to be delivered.

---

14. What do they need more of?
    - (A) Hangers
    - (B) Pillows
    - (C) Soap
    - (D) Towels

15. What was the speaker going to do?
    - (A) Go shopping
    - (B) Call the front desk
    - (C) Write a letter
    - (D) Go dancing

16. What is probably true?
    - (A) They are not in their room yet.
    - (B) They have eaten dinner.
    - (C) They plan to exchange some money.
    - (D) Everyone has not yet arrived to the room.

PART IV: Short Talks ((Track 161))

You will hear two talks, each followed by three questions. Listen carefully, and choose the best answer to each question.

17. Which is true?
    (A) The guest is alone.
    (B) The guest did not make a reservation.
    (C) The guest is leaving early.
    (D) The guest is with two friends.

18. When is this information given?
    (A) At check-out time
    (B) Any time people take the elevator
    (C) During check-in
    (D) When the hotel gift shop closes

19. What instructions are given?
    (A) How to get out if there is a fire
    (B) How to find good souvenirs
    (C) How to take the shuttle bus
    (D) How to unlock the door

---

20. Why is the hotel full?
    (A) A convention is in town.
    (B) It is the best hotel in town.
    (C) It is the peak season.
    (D) The hotel is very small.

21. How many people will share the room?
    (A) Two
    (B) Three
    (C) Four
    (D) Five

22. What will they probably do?
    (A) Change hotels
    (B) Change the reservation
    (C) Reserve an additional room
    (D) Request an additional bed

UNIT 8 Transportation

Warm-up

A

Look & Listen

Listen to the dialogs. ((Track 162))

B

Listen Again

Listen again, and fill in the blanks. ((Track 163))

1. The man will leave for _____ at _____.
2. The man will leave for _____ in _____.
3. The man's bus arrived at _____, which was _____.
4. The woman is taking the _____ bus to _____.

Essential Expressions

Write the missing words to make correct expressions.

a bike	a bus	a cab or taxi	a camel	a car
a carriage	a motor boat	a train	an airplane	the subway

Transportation for less than 20 people	**Transportation for more than 20 people**
_____ _____	_____ _____
_____ _____	_____ _____
_____ _____	_____ _____

Listening Practice

A

How would you answer?

Listen. Write the answer. ((Track 164))

| About two hours. | No, I'm afraid not. | They're $175 each. |
| At 11:20 a.m. | Yes, we are. | |

1. _____
2. _____
3. _____
4. _____
5. _____

B

How would you ask?

Listen. Write the question. ((Track 165))

| Economy or first class? | Has it arrived yet? | Is the flight full? |
| May I see your tickets? | When will we arrive? | |

1. _____
2. _____
3. _____
4. _____
5. _____

C

Picture Description

Describe the picture using the words below.

| full | handle | subway | crowded |

✓ Listen to the description of the picture. ((Track 166))

Speaking Practice

A

Pronunciation
Practice

In casual speech, you may hear the phrase "going to" pronounced as "gonna."

Written	Spoken
1. Is the flight going to be delayed?	1. Is the flight gonna be delayed?
2. My bus is going to depart soon.	2. My bus is gonna depart soon.
3. We are going to have to wait an hour.	3. We're gonna have to wait an hour.

✓ **Now practice saying the following sentences.**

1. It is going to arrive in twenty minutes.
2. We are going to rent a car.
3. How are we going to get there?

✓ **Now listen and repeat.** (((Track 167)))

B

Conversation
Pictures

Listen to the dialogs, and number the pictures. (((Track 168)))

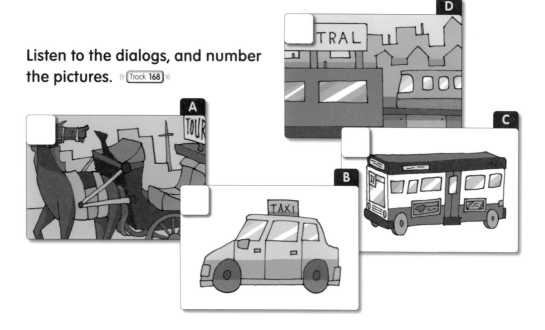

✓ **Now listen to the dialogs again, and choose the correct destination for each person.**

1. (A) Rockford Center   (B) The airport   (C) The park   (D) The stadium
2. (A) Rockford Center   (B) The airport   (C) The park   (D) The stadium
3. (A) Rockford Center   (B) The airport   (C) The park   (D) The stadium
4. (A) Rockford Center   (B) The airport   (C) The park   (D) The stadium

Short Dialogs

A
Dialog 1

Listen to the dialog and questions. Choose the best answer. ((Track 169))

1. (A) Easy traveling
   (C) Save money

   (B) Flexible schedule
   (D) Save time

2. (A) A complicated schedule
   (C) The people on the train

   (B) Bad past experience
   (D) The route the train follows

✓ **Listen again, and fill in the blanks.**

W: We could take a bus, we could ❶_____,
   or we could take the train.

M: The ❷_____ is the cheapest way to go,
   but it will take a ❸_____ to get there.

W: Right. I'd rather not take the ❹_____, either.

M: Why not?

W: The last time I took the ❺_____, I lost my
   ❻_____ and got sick from the food.

B
Dialog 2

Listen to the dialog and questions. Choose the best answer. ((Track 170))

1. (A) The Amazon
   (C) The Nile

   (B) The Mississippi
   (D) The Thames

2. (A) Exciting
   (C) Difficult

   (B) Scary
   (D) Boring

C
Dialog 3

Listen to the dialog, and write the missing information on the map. ((Track 171))

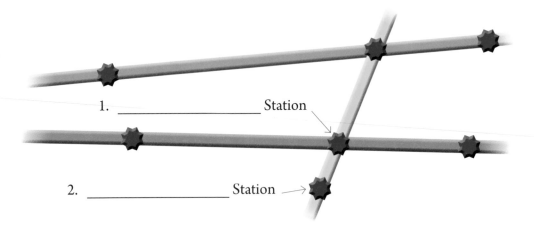

1. _____ Station

2. _____ Station

A
Listen

Listen to the dialog, and choose the best answer. ((Track 172))

1. Which is true about the man's reservation?
    (A) It was changed.
    (B) It is on the computer.
    (C) It is not on the computer.
    (D) It does not have his name on it.

2. How many days will the man keep the car?
    (A) One
    (B) Three
    (C) Seven
    (D) Ten

3. What will the man buy?
    (A) Fuel
    (B) Keys
    (C) Insurance
    (D) Mileage

B
Listen Again

Listen again, and fill in the blanks. ((Track 173))

W: How may I help you?

M: I have a reservation to ❶_____ a car under the name of Johnson.

W: Let me just ❷_____ that file, Mr. Johnson. Robert Johnson?

M: Yes, that's right. I reserved a mid-sized car for ❸_____ days.

W: I have your reservation ❹_____ here, Mr. Johnson. A mid-sized car for ❺_____ days with unlimited mileage. Would you like to pay for us to fill up the ❻_____ when you bring it back? Or do you want to buy the ❼_____ yourself before you turn in the car?

M: I'll pay for the ❽_____ now so I don't have to worry about ❾_____ it up.

W: Alright, Mr. Johnson. Please ❿_____ on the bottom line and write your initials here.

Short Talks

Listen to the short talk and questions. Choose the best answer. ((Track 174))

1. (A) Number of helicopters   (B) Places to stop
   (C) Scheduled flights per day   (D) Years offering tours

2. (A) Boat tours   (B) Bus tours
   (C) Hiking tours   (D) Tours on horseback

✓ **Listen again, and fill in the blanks.**

Skyview Grand Canyon Helicopter Tours is the most
❶_____ helicopter company serving
❷_____ to Las Vegas and the Grand Canyon.
In addition to helicopter tours, Skyview also offers
❸_____ tour packages to the South Rim. As
always, our ❹_____ is dedicated to the comfort
and ❺_____ of our passengers. Rely on Skyview
for a spectacular ❻_____ from liftoff to touchdown.

Listen to the short talk and questions. Choose the best answer. ((Track 175))

1. (A) A bus   (B) A jeep
   (C) A truck   (D) A van

2. (A) Riding an elephant   (B) Riding a horse
   (C) Riding a motorcycle   (D) Riding a ship

Listen to the short talk, and complete each statement. ((Track 176))

1. The speaker is a _____ driver.

2. He takes customers through the _____.

3. A man and a woman together only need to pay _____.

Listening Quiz

Listen to the dialogs. Choose the correct picture. (((Track 177)))

 **A**

 **B**

 **C**

1. (A)   (B)   (C)

2. (A)   (B)   (C)

Listen to the dialogs and questions. Choose the best answer. (((Track 178)))

3. (A) Before 7:30   (B) After 7:30
   (C) Always   (D) Never

4. (A) Embarrassment   (B) Nervousness
   (C) Sadness   (D) Surprise

5. (A) Go shopping   (B) Meet her mother
   (C) See a painting   (D) Stay home

6. (A) Less than ten minutes   (B) Less than half an hour
   (C) Over an hour   (D) All day

7. (A) By boat   (B) By foot
   (C) By helicopter   (D) By horseback

8. (A) On an airplane   (B) On a boat
   (C) On a bus   (D) In a taxi

9. (A) It is dangerous.   (B) It is normal.
   (C) It is slow.   (D) It is too heavy.

Wrap-up

A
Pre-listening Discussion

Talk about these questions.

1. Do you enjoy traveling by train? Why or why not?
2. What is the longest trip you have taken by train?
3. What do you know about the Trans-Siberian Railroad?

B
Listening Comprehension

Listen and answer the questions. ((Track 179))

1. **Who had the idea to build the Trans-Siberian Railroad?**
   _____ had the idea to build the Trans-Siberian Railroad.

2. **How many years did it take to complete the railroad?**
   It took _____ years to complete the railroad.

3. **How long does it take to travel by train from Moscow to Vladivostok?**
   It takes _____ to travel by train from Moscow to Vladivostok.

C
Dictation Practice

Listen again, and fill in the blanks. ((Track 180))

In 1860, the ❶_____ of Vladivostok was ❷_____. This was a very ❸_____ city for Russia because ❹_____ only a few years, it ❺_____ Russia's largest port city ❻_____ the Pacific. However, there ❼_____ a huge distance between ❽_____ and Vladivostok, and sending ❾_____ across the country was ❿_____. The tsar, Alexander III, ⓫_____ a railroad to ⓬_____ the European and Asian ⓭_____ of Russia, and in ⓮_____, work on the Trans-Siberian ⓯_____ began.

It took decades to ⓰_____ the railroad. Convicts and ⓱_____ were put to work ⓲_____ both ends of the ⓳_____ working toward the center. ⓴_____ 1898, trains could run ㉑_____ either end of the ㉒_____ to Lake Baikal, but the ㉓_____ still blocked completion ㉔_____ the line. Lake Baikal ㉕_____ more than 600 kilometers ㉖_____ and over 1,800 meters ㉗_____. The only way to ㉘_____ passengers and cargo ㉙_____ the lake was by ㉚_____ until a special line ㉛_____ be built around the southern ㉜_____ of the lake.

The Trans-Siberian ㉝_____ was finally completed in ㉞_____, connecting Vladivostok in the ㉟_____ with Petrograd in the ㊱_____. Both passengers and cargo ㊲_____ still transported today ㊳_____ the railroad, with the ㊴_____ km trip from Moscow ㊵_____ Vladivostok taking ㊶_____ days.

Listening Test 🕗 08:39

PART I: Picture Description ((Track 181))

Listen and choose the statement that best describes what you see in the picture.

1.

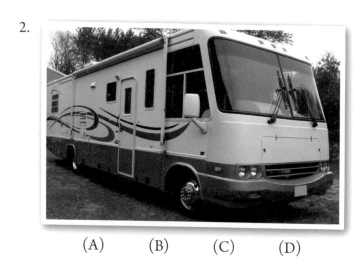

(A)   (B)   (C)   (D)

2.

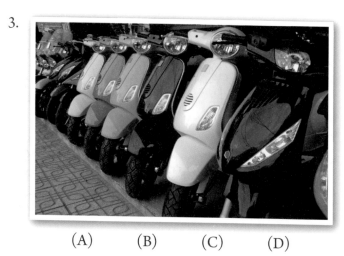

(A)   (B)   (C)   (D)

3.

(A)   (B)   (C)   (D)

4.

(A)   (B)   (C)   (D)

5.

(A)   (B)   (C)   (D)

PART II: Questions and Responses ((Track 182))

Listen and choose the best response to each question.

6. (A)   (B)   (C)

7. (A)   (B)   (C)

8. (A)   (B)   (C)

9. (A)   (B)   (C)

10. (A)   (B)   (C)

PART III: Short Conversations ((Track 183))

You will hear two dialogs, each followed by three questions. Listen carefully, and choose the best answer to each question.

11. Why does the man suggest taking a later train?

    (A) So they can sit down

    (B) To get there faster

    (C) So they won't arrive too early

    (D) To save money

12. What was the woman's reply?

    (A) Any train would be fine.

    (B) She wanted to take the fast train.

    (C) They should take a bus instead.

    (D) The first train had a more scenic view.

13. What did the man remind the woman about?

    (A) Next week's party

    (B) An appointment

    (C) Her exam results

    (D) A marriage proposal

---

14. What is the man requesting?

    (A) His departure time

    (B) His food preference

    (C) His seat location

    (D) His travel date

15. What did the agent ask the man?

    (A) If he would like a seat in the back

    (B) If he would prefer a vegetarian meal

    (C) If he would like the only window seat left

    (D) If he would let another passenger go by

16. Where are the speakers NOT located?

    (A) An airport

    (B) A train station

    (C) A classroom

    (D) A bus depot

PART IV: Short Talks ((Track 184))

You will hear two talks, each followed by three questions. Listen carefully, and choose the best answer to each question.

17. Why won't the driver take the highway?

    (A) She doesn't like to drive fast.
    (B) The passenger wants to see sights.
    (C) The road is icy.
    (D) There is a traffic jam.

18. Where is the driver trying to go?

    (A) To the airport
    (B) To a hotel
    (C) To the park
    (D) To a theater

19. What is the benefit of taking Lemon Avenue?

    (A) Fewer cars
    (B) Lots of interesting houses
    (C) Many broken traffic lights
    (D) No speed limit

---

20. Which kind of transportation is he promoting?

    (A) Carriage rides
    (B) Deluxe taxi service
    (C) Limousine service
    (D) Shuttle bus

21. What is the man's key selling point?

    (A) Convenience
    (B) Free extras
    (C) Quick service
    (D) Romance

22. Where is the man?

    (A) At a subway
    (B) In the park
    (C) In a garage
    (D) In a post office

Banks

Warm-up

Listen to the dialogs. ((Track 185))

Listen again, and write the word that fits the description. ((Track 186))

1. This is needed in order to make a withdrawal: _____
2. This can be used to check how much is in your bank account: _____
3. The lady at the desk can help you with this: _____
4. This is where you can change foreign money into American money: _____

Write the missing words to make correct sentences.

balance	cash	check	credit	deposit
exchange	loan	savings	transfer	withdrawal

1. I don't have enough cash, so I'll write a _____ for my purchase.
2. Can I check the _____ of my account using an ATM machine?
3. Do you know the _____ rate for US dollars into British pounds?
4. Every month, I try to put at least $20 into my _____ account for the future.
5. I need to make a _____ of $50 from my account.
6. She got paid today, so she went to the bank to _____ her paycheck.
7. Visa and Mastercard are two kinds of major _____ cards.
8. It's easy to apply for a _____.
9. You can _____ money from your savings to your checking account online.
10. Instead of putting this money into my account, I'll just _____ the check because I need some spending money.

Listening Practice

Listen. Write the answer. ((Track 187))

| On this line right here. | No, I'm afraid we don't. |
| The fee is ten dollars per month. | No, it's not.   Yes. It's $500.75. |

1. _____
2. _____
3. _____
4. _____
5. _____

Listen. Write the question. ((Track 188))

How would you like that?	What is today's exchange rate?
When does the bank open?	Where is the nearest ATM machine?
Will you take a credit card?	

1. _____
2. _____
3. _____
4. _____
5. _____

Describe the picture using the words below.

| clients   interior   accounts   transactions |
| _____ |
| _____ |
| _____ |
| _____ |

✓ **Listen to the description of the picture.** ((Track 189))

Speaking Practice

A

Intonation Practice

In certain three-syllable statements or questions, the stress should be on the first syllable. Say the following statements and questions using the stress pattern "da dum dum."

Written	Spoken
1. I don't know.	1. **I** don't.
2. Show me one.	2. **Show** me one.
3. Coins are fine.	3. **Coins** are fine.

✓ Now practice saying the following phrases. Remember to stress the first syllable.

1. PIN number
2. Wait a sec.
3. Sign this, please.

✓ Now listen and repeat. ((Track 190))

B

Conversation Pictures

Listen to the dialogs, and number the pictures. ((Track 191))

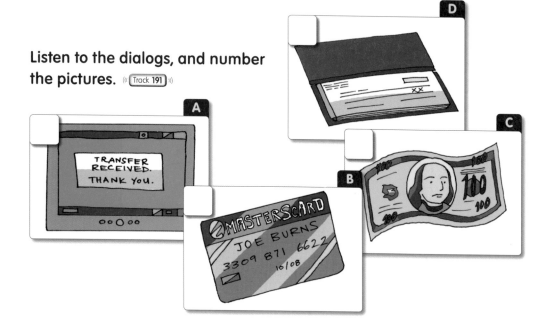

✓ Now listen to the dialogs again, and choose the correct amount.

1. (A) $3.50   (B) $18   (C) $32   (D) $500
2. (A) $3.50   (B) $18   (C) $32   (D) $500
3. (A) $3.50   (B) $18   (C) $32   (D) $500
4. (A) $3.50   (B) $18   (C) $32   (D) $500

Short Dialogs

Dialog 1

Listen to the dialog and questions. Choose the best answer. ((Track 192))

1. (A) Checking
   (C) Savings
   (B) College
   (D) Stock

2. (A) Put in some money
   (C) Take out some money
   (B) Put in the same amount of money
   (D) Take out all of her money

✓ **Listen again, and fill in the blanks.**

M: What did you do with the money you got for your ❶_____?

W: I put it in my ❷_____ account.

M: Do you have a lot of money ❸_____ in your account?

W: ❹_____. I started my savings account last year. But my father said he would ❺_____ the amount I saved by ❻_____ at the end of the year.

Dialog 2

Listen to the dialog and questions. Choose the best answer. ((Track 193))

1. (A) Go to the bank
   (C) Use a computer
   (B) Talk to a teller
   (D) Work in a bank

2. (A) Account
   (C) ID
   (B) Gift card
   (D) Telephone

Dialog 3

Listen to the dialog, and check (✓) the information that can be inferred from what is said. ((Track 194))

1. ☐ She went to an ATM machine already.

   ☐ She is looking for an ATM machine.

2. ☐ There is no money in her account.

   ☐ There is not a problem with the machine.

Main Dialog

Listen to the dialog, and choose the best answer. ((Track 195))

1. What day is it?
   - (A) Friday
   - (B) Saturday
   - (C) Sunday
   - (D) Monday

2. What kind of card does the man have?
   - (A) Bank card
   - (B) Gift card
   - (C) ID card
   - (D) Savings card

3. Which number does the man not know?
   - (A) His account number
   - (B) His balance
   - (C) His bank's ID number
   - (D) His PIN number

Listen again, and fill in the blanks. ((Track 196))

M: Hmm. I should probably make a withdrawal. Oh, no! I can't believe this.

W: What's the matter?

M: Well, take a look. This bank is ❶_____!

W: Didn't you know that? This branch is always closed on ❷_____.

M: No, I didn't know. The bank in my area of town never closes on a Saturday. What am I going to do? I don't have any ❸_____.

W: You do have a ❹_____ card, don't you? You could get some ❺_____ from an ATM machine.

M: I have a ❻_____ card, but I've never used it. I don't even remember what my ❼_____ number is.

W: Well, I guess I can ❽_____ you some cash until ❾_____. Come on. I'll make a withdrawal from that ❿_____.

Short Talks

A
Short Talk 1

Listen to the short talk and questions. Choose the best answer. ((Track 197))

1. (A) Always ask for a discount.
   (B) Invest in stocks.
   (C) Put money in the bank.
   (D) Work while you are young.

2. (A) 5 percent
   (B) 10 percent
   (C) 20 percent
   (D) 50 percent

✓ **Listen again, and fill in the blanks.**

Here is a good piece of advice: Start ❶_____
money when you are young. Another good rule to follow is to
try and save ❷_____ of everything you earn. So
if your parents give you ❸_____ for cleaning the
house, save ❹_____ cents. When you are older
and have a real job, keep saving ❺_____ from
every paycheck. If you do that, you won't have to worry
about ❻_____ when you are older.

B
Short Talk 2

Listen to the short talk, and questions. Choose the best answer. ((Track 198))

1. (A) A man
   (B) A police officer
   (C) Another robber
   (D) A woman

2. (A) At the airport
   (B) In the bank
   (C) In his house
   (D) On the street

C
Short Talk 3

Listen to the short talk and number the steps in order from 1-4. ((Track 199))

_____ (A) Fill in the amount
_____ (B) Put the date
_____ (C) Sign the check
_____ (D) Write the name

Listening Quiz 03:54

A

Picture Matching

Listen to the dialogs. Choose the correct picture. ((Track 200))

A	**B**	**C**

1. (A)   (B)   (C)

2. (A)   (B)   (C)

B

Listen & Choose

Listen to the dialogs and questions. Choose the best answer. ((Track 201))

3. (A) Asking for advice   (B) Giving directions
   (C) Paying her bill   (D) Using an ATM machine

4. (A) A checking account   (B) A credit card
   (C) A safety deposit box   (D) A savings account

5. (A) Her account is empty.   (B) Her application will be accepted.
   (C) She already applied.   (D) She can't apply.

6. (A) Apply for a loan   (B) Buy a car
   (C) Deposit his check   (D) Work in a bank

7. (A) Wait until next week   (B) Transfer some money
   (C) Open a new account   (D) Get money from her parents

8. (A) Closing her account   (B) Exchanging foreign money
   (C) Putting money into her account   (D) Taking money out of her account

9. (A) A pen   (B) A receipt
   (C) An application form   (D) Cash

Wrap-up

Talk about these questions.

1. Can you name the kind of money used in five other countries?
2. Which of these currencies is the most/least valuable?
3. Do you know the exchange rate of dollars and the currency in your country?

Listen and answer the questions. (((Track 202)))

1. **When did countries start to use the Euro as currency?**
   Countries started using the Euro as currency in _____.

2. **How many countries used the Euro in 2002?**
   In 2002, _____ countries used the Euro.

3. **What was the average exchange rate of Euros and US dollars between 2002 and 2006?**
   The average exchange rate of Euros and US dollars between 2002 and 2006 was
   _____.

Listen again, and fill in the blanks. (((Track 203)))

Unless you travel ❶_____, you probably don't ❷_____ about the value of ❸_____ in your country. In ❹_____ words, most people don't ❺_____ much attention to exchange ❻_____ in their daily lives. ❼_____, international businesses and ❽_____ pay a lot of ❾_____ to exchange rates.

In ❿_____ of 2002, an interesting ⓫_____ happened to exchange rates in ⓬_____. The exchange rates in ⓭_____ European countries disappeared! ⓮_____ happened because those ⓯_____ countries started using the ⓰_____ as currency. The countries ⓱_____ Belgium, Denmark, Finland, Luxembourg, ⓲_____, Portugal, Greece, Austria, France, ⓳_____, Germany, and Spain.

At the ⓴_____, one Euro was almost ㉑_____ to one dollar in the ㉒_____ States. So for people ㉓_____ between those European ㉔_____ and the United States, ㉕_____ was easy to see ㉖_____ products were more or ㉗_____ expensive in each place. Of ㉘_____, exchange rates do not ㉙_____ the same for very ㉚_____. In fact, they change ㉛_____ about every day! However, ㉜_____ one looks at the ㉝_____ exchange rates between dollars ㉞_____ Euros over several years, ㉟_____ wasn't much change. Between 2002 and ㊱_____, the average exchange rate ㊲_____ close to one Euro ㊳_____ one US dollar. The ㊴_____ over those five years was actually 1.2 Euros ㊵_____ US dollar.

PART I: Picture Description ((Track 204))

Listen and choose the statement that best describes what you see in the picture.

1.

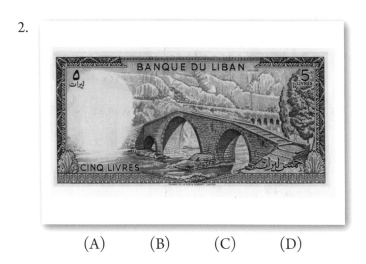

(A)   (B)   (C)   (D)

2.

(A)   (B)   (C)   (D)

3.

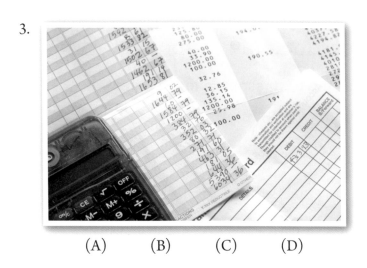

(A)   (B)   (C)   (D)

4.

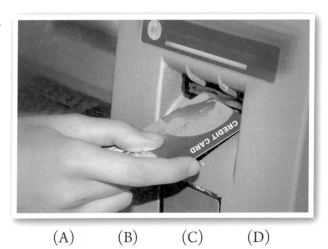

(A)   (B)   (C)   (D)

5.

(A)   (B)   (C)   (D)

PART II: Questions and Responses ((Track 205))

Listen and choose the best response to each question.

6. (A)   (B)   (C)

7. (A)   (B)   (C)

8. (A)   (B)   (C)

9. (A)   (B)   (C)

10. (A)   (B)   (C)

PART III: Short Conversations ((Track 206))

You will hear two dialogs, each followed by three questions. Listen carefully, and choose the best answer to each question.

11. How much money does the woman have?
    - (A) Less than $5
    - (B) Less than $10
    - (C) One $20 bill
    - (D) One

12. What did the woman forget to do?
    - (A) Go to the bank
    - (B) Write a check
    - (C) Pay a bill
    - (D) Meet a friend

13. What was the woman's response to the offer?
    - (A) She didn't want anything.
    - (B) She didn't want that much money.
    - (C) She wanted to get more.
    - (D) She didn't believe it.

---

14. What did the woman do?
    - (A) She deposited money.
    - (B) She exchanged money.
    - (C) She transferred money.
    - (D) She withdrew money.

15. What was the purpose of the money?
    - (A) To pay a credit card bill
    - (B) To pay a utility bill
    - (C) To put in a scholarship fund
    - (D) To loan a friend

16. What does the man hope for next year?
    - (A) To go on a nice vacation
    - (B) To transfer more money to his checking account
    - (C) To open a new account
    - (D) To pay off a credit card bill

PART IV: Short Talks ((Track 207))

You will hear two talks, each followed by three questions. Listen carefully, and choose the best answer to each question.

17. Who does this advice apply to?
    - (A) People with a lot of money
    - (B) People without credit cards
    - (C) People who don't have jobs
    - (D) People working in banks

18. What kind of card should people get first?
    - (A) An ID card
    - (B) A gas station card
    - (C) An insurance card
    - (D) A major credit card

19. Which is a key point in this advice?
    - (A) Make as many cards as possible
    - (B) Never use the cards
    - (C) Only use the cards to buy expensive items
    - (D) Use the cards and pay the bills

---

20. What is the speaker's problem?
    - (A) He has no money.
    - (B) He has less money than he thought.
    - (C) He has more money than he thought.
    - (D) He lost his wallet.

21. What happened to the money?
    - (A) He found it in his pocket.
    - (B) He gave it to a friend.
    - (C) He has more money than he thought.
    - (D) He spent it.

22. What did the speaker do yesterday?
    - (A) Work at the mall
    - (B) Ride the bus
    - (C) Borrow $20 from a friend
    - (D) Watch a movie

10 Driving

Warm-up

A
Look & Listen

Listen to the dialogs. ((Track 208))

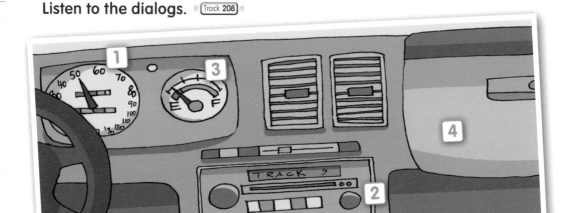

B
Listen Again

Listen again, and fill in the blanks. ((Track 209))

1. The speed limit near the _____ is _____ kph.
2. They are listening to track _____ on the CD, but there are _____ tracks in all.
3. The car is low on _____, so she will put in _____ liters.
4. In the glove box, he finds a map of the _____ and a map of the _____.

C
Essential Expressions

Write the missing words to make correct sentences.

| no-parking | fill up | speed limit | have | pull over |
| put it in | put on | roll down | take | turn on |

1. You can _____ the glove box.
2. Please _____ your seatbelt.
3. Do you _____ a spare tire in the trunk?
4. I think this is a _____ zone.
5. Should I _____ the air conditioner?
6. Let's _____ the gas tank.
7. I'm going to _____ the highway.
8. Slow down. Just go the _____.
9. Do you mind if I _____ the window?
10. We'll have to _____ to the side.

Listening Practice

How would you answer?

Listen. Write the answer. (Track 210)

A Volkswagen.	It's eighty.	About three hours.
It's six years old.	At the next street.	

1. _____

2. _____

3. _____

4. _____

5. _____

B

How would you ask?

Listen. Write the question or statement. (Track 211)

I can give you a ride.	What kind of car is it?	Is this a new car?
I think you're driving too fast.	Does the air conditioner work?	

1. _____

2. _____

3. _____

4. _____

5. _____

C

Picture Description

Describe the picture using the words below.

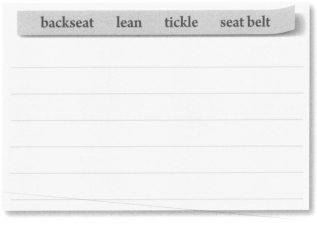

backseat	lean	tickle	seat belt

_____

_____

_____

_____

✓ **Listen to the description of the picture.** (Track 212)

Speaking Practice

A

Pronunciation Practice

In casual speech, you may hear the phrases "should have," "could have," and "would have" pronounced as "shoulda, "coulda," and "woulda."

Written	Spoken
1. We should have stopped for gas.	1. We shoulda stopped for gas.
2. I could have turned there.	2. I coulda turned there.
3. He would have parked closer if you asked him to.	3. He woulda parked closer if you asked him to.

✓ **Now practice saying the following sentences.**

1. You could have put your bag in the trunk.
2. I should have pulled over after we got off the highway.
3. She would have turned on the air conditioner, but it didn't work.

✓ **Now listen and repeat.** ((Track 213))

B

Conversation Pictures

Listen to the dialogs, and number the pictures. ((Track 214))

✓ **Now listen to the dialogs again, and choose the correct place they will go next.**

1. (A) Bakery (B) Gas station (C) Highway (D) Home
2. (A) Bakery (B) Gas station (C) Highway (D) Home
3. (A) Bakery (B) Gas station (C) Highway (D) Home
4. (A) Bakery (B) Gas station (C) Highway (D) Home

Dialog 1

Listen to the dialog and questions. Choose the best answer. ((Track 215))

1. (A) His car
   (C) His foot
   (B) His eyes
   (D) His teeth

2. (A) A limousine
   (C) An antique car
   (B) A manual
   (D) An automatic

✓ **Listen again, and fill in the blanks.**

M: Can you drive me home tomorrow after my
   ❶_____ doctor's appointment?

W: It depends. What ❷_____ is your
   appointment?

M: It's at ❸_____ in the afternoon.

W: That's fine. I don't work until
   ❹_____ tomorrow evening.

M: Do you know how to ❺_____ a
   car with a stick shift?

W: Yes, I do. My first car was a ❻_____.

Dialog 2

Listen to the dialog and questions. Choose the best answer. ((Track 216))

1. (A) Drive slowly
   (C) Turn off the radio
   (B) Put on glasses
   (D) Wear a seat belt

2. (A) Confused
   (C) Happy
   (B) Excited
   (D) Worried

C

Dialog 3

Listen to the dialog and questions. Complete the answers. ((Track 217))

1. The woman is _____.

2. She needs to _____.

Main Dialog

Listen to the dialog, and choose the best answer. ((Track 218))

1. What does the man think about the driver of the other car?
   (A) He is cool.   (B) He is dangerous.
   (C) He is funny.   (D) He is rude.

2. What does the woman think about the other driver's action?
   (A) It is annoying.   (B) It is brave.
   (C) It is OK.   (D) It is polite.

3. What does the man think the other driver should do?
   (A) Change lanes   (B) Slow down
   (C) Stop his car   (D) Use his horn

Listen again, and fill in the blanks. ((Track 219))

M: Hey, look at that man in the ❶_____ next to us!

W: I can't look at him now. You know that I'm ❷_____. Just tell me, what's he doing?

M: Well, he's ❸_____ and talking on his cell phone at the ❹_____ time.

W: Is that all? I see people driving and talking on cell phones all the time.

M: I know, but it's ❺_____. He could easily get distracted and wind up having an accident. If he needs to talk on his cell phone, he should ❻_____ and stop before he ❼_____ the phone.

W: Well, you're being a little judgmental, don't you think? Don't you ever ❽_____ on your cell phone while you're ❾_____?

M: Actually, I don't ❿_____ a cell phone.

Short Talks

Listen to the short talk and questions. Choose the best answer. ((Track 220))

1. (A) To ask for information
   (C) To give directions
   (B) To explain a problem
   (D) To plan a trip

2. (A) Buena Vista
   (C) Red Tile
   (B) Gardenia
   (D) Ridgecrest

✓ **Listen again, and fill in the blanks.**

Hi, Brenda. I guess you're not ❶_____ right now. I was calling to explain how to get to ❷_____ for the party on Friday night. Go ❸_____ Buena Vista Boulevard to Gardenia Drive. Turn ❹_____ onto Gardenia. The second street on the ❺_____ will be Ridgecrest. Turn there, and my house is the second house ❻_____. It's the house with the red tiles on the roof.

Listen to the short talk and questions. Choose the best answer. ((Track 221))

1. (A) One day
   (C) Five days
   (B) Two days
   (D) Ten days

2. (A) One hour
   (C) Six hours
   (B) Two hours
   (D) Eight hours

Listen to the short talk, and circle the parts of the car that the speaker mentions. ((Track 222))

back seat

gas tank

glove box

seat belt

steering wheel

trunk

Listening Quiz

03:34

Listen to the dialogs. Choose the correct picture. ((Track 223))

A

B

C

1. (A)　　　　(B)　　　　(C)

2. (A)　　　　(B)　　　　(C)

Listen to the dialogs and questions. Choose the best answer. ((Track 224))

3. (A) It can go fast. (B) It has a big trunk.
   (C) It is a pretty color. (D) It uses little gas.

4. (A) A new battery (B) A new tire
   (C) More gas (D) More water

5. (A) A sign (B) Paint on the curb
   (C) The line on the street (D) The police officer

6. (A) Cold (B) Hot
   (C) Rainy (D) Windy

7. (A) Ask for directions (B) Roll down the windows
   (C) Stop the car (D) Turn on the air conditioner

8. (A) A taxi driver (B) The man
   (C) The woman (D) Their father

9. (A) It is not on the map. (B) It is one way.
   (C) There is too much traffic. (D) They have a flat tire.

Wrap-up

Talk about these questions.

1. Do you have any friends or relatives with small children? Do they also have car seats?
2. How often did you ride in a child car seat when you were very young?
3. Until what age should children in cars ride in child car seats?

Listen and answer the questions. (((Track 225)))

1. **How many types of car seats are described by the speaker?**
   The speaker described _____ types of car seats.

2. **When should a child start using a forward-facing car seat?**
   A child should start using a forward-facing car seat when she or he is _____
   _____.

3. **Why should a five-year-old child use a booster seat?**
   A five-year-old child should use a booster seat so that _____
   _____.

Listen again, and fill in the blanks. (((Track 226)))

Most people know the ❶_____ of wearing seat belts, especially
❷_____ people in the front ❸_____ of a car. Even ❹_____ at just
45 kph, a ❺_____ can be seriously hurt ❻_____ an accident. But seat belts
❼_____ designed for adults. When ❽_____ ride in a car, ❾_____ should
sit in child ❿_____ seats for their safety. ⓫_____ are three kinds of ⓬_____
seats, and each should ⓭_____ used by children of ⓮_____ ages.

When babies ⓯_____ in a car, they ⓰_____ sit in a car seat ⓱_____
the rear of the ⓲_____. Usually these car seats ⓳_____ like small beds. The
⓴_____ can lie in the car ㉑_____ and look out the ㉒_____ window
of the car. ㉓_____ rear-facing car seats ㉔_____ made for children up to
㉕_____ months old or children ㉖_____ ten kilograms.

When a ㉗_____ is over twelve months ㉘_____, they can sit in a
㉙_____ seat facing the front ㉚_____. In these seats, the ㉛_____ sits
in the same ㉜_____ other passengers in the car ㉝_____. But rather than
have a ㉞_____ across the child's lap ㉟_____ chest, these car seats
㊱_____ special belts to ㊲_____ the child better in an ㊳_____.

Once a child grows ㊴_____ big to fit in ㊵_____ or her car seat, the
㊶_____ should use a "booster" ㊷_____. This is like a ㊸_____ seat that
boosts the ㊹_____ up so that a ㊺_____ seat belt fits correctly ㊻_____
the child. Booster seats ㊼_____ be used until a ㊽_____ is at least ㊾_____
years old.

Listening Test

PART I: Picture Description ((Track 227))

Listen and choose the statement that best describes what you see in the picture.

1.

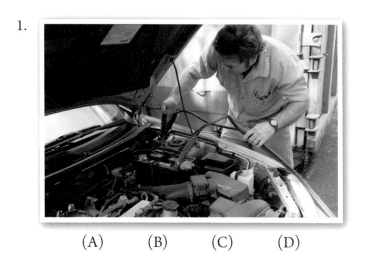

　　　(A)　　　(B)　　　(C)　　　(D)

2.

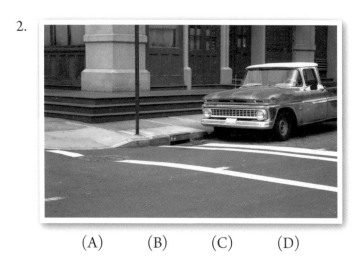

　　　(A)　　　(B)　　　(C)　　　(D)

3.

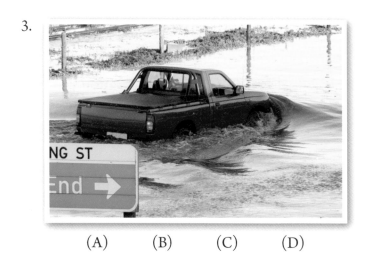

　　　(A)　　　(B)　　　(C)　　　(D)

4.

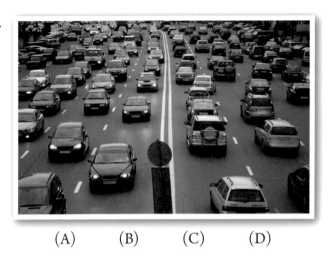

(A)   (B)   (C)   (D)

5.

(A)   (B)   (C)   (D)

PART II: Questions and Responses ((Track 228))

Listen and choose the best response to each question.

6. (A)   (B)   (C)

7. (A)   (B)   (C)

8. (A)   (B)   (C)

9. (A)   (B)   (C)

10. (A)   (B)   (C)

PART III: Short Conversations ((Track 229))

You will hear two dialogs, each followed by three questions. Listen carefully, and choose the best answer to each question.

11. What is the problem?

    (A) The driver feels sick.

    (B) The car is moving too slowly.

    (C) The car is making an unusual sound.

    (D) The passenger is angry.

12. Where are the speakers?

    (A) In a garage

    (B) In a car

    (C) In a house

    (D) In a driveway

13. Where does the woman want to go?

    (A) A restaurant

    (B) A car mechanic

    (C) A gas station

    (D) A car wash

---

14. What was the man's problem?

    (A) He is lost again.

    (B) He lost his license.

    (C) He cannot find his keys.

    (D) He can never drive.

15. What does the woman suggest?

    (A) Put important things in the same place

    (B) Keep better track of things

    (C) Always give her important items

    (D) Don't forget to go to the post office

16. Where are they?

    (A) In a gas station

    (B) In a train station

    (C) At an office

    (D) At a home

PART IV: Short Talks (((Track 230)))

You will hear two talks, each followed by three questions. Listen carefully, and choose the best answer to each question.

17. What is this advice for?

    (A) How to sleep well
    (B) What is the best music
    (C) Where to find good rest areas
    (D) How to avoid accidents

18. When would this advice be useful?

    (A) Driving to another city
    (B) Driving to work
    (C) Going to a concert
    (D) If you cannot sleep

19. What is NOT a suggestion the speaker makes?

    (A) To listen to energetic music
    (B) To stretch and walk around
    (C) To get enough sleep the night before
    (D) To turn on the air conditioning

---

20. What is true about the younger brother?

    (A) He often drives too slow.
    (B) He never goes through stop signs.
    (C) He is a bad driver.
    (D) He cannot drive yet.

21. Why is one brother a bad driver?

    (A) He does not follow rules.
    (B) He has many accidents.
    (C) He likes loud music.
    (D) He is too young.

22. What is true about the older brother?

    (A) He pays more attention to music than the road.
    (B) He always stops at red lights.
    (C) He sometimes drives too fast on the highway.
    (D) He drives like his younger brother.

A

Look & Listen

Warm-up

Listen to the dialogs. ((Track 231))

B

Listen Again

Listen again, and match the place with the direction. ((Track 232))

1. Picnic table   •   • (A) Here by the front door
2. Room   •   • (B) Out in the backyard
3. Bathroom   •   • (C) Down the hall on the left
4. Closet   •   • (D) Upstairs

C

Essential Expressions

Circle the right answer for each question.

1. How big is the house next door to your house?
   (A) It's a two-story.   (B) It's unfurnished.

2. When will you be able to move in?
   (A) This is the master bedroom.   (B) Probably next weekend.

3. Did you buy the apartment?
   (A) No, we're just renting.   (B) On the third floor.

4. Why do you want to live in the dormitory?
   (A) Because I forgot the address.   (B) It's more convenient.

5. Does the apartment come with furniture in it?
   (A) No, it's unfurnished.   (B) Put it in the living room.

Listening Practice

Listen. Write the answer. ((Track 233))

> 1904 Timberlake Drive.   It has three.   No, it doesn't.
> It's on the fifth floor.   Yes, there are.

1. _____
2. _____
3. _____
4. _____
5. _____

Listen. Write the question. ((Track 234))

> Does the bathroom have a tub?   Who lives next door to you?
> Have you always lived in an apartment?
> Is your bedroom upstairs?   Where do you live?

1. _____
2. _____
3. _____
4. _____
5. _____

Describe the picture using the words below.

yard	agent	sign	front porch

_____

_____

_____

_____

✓ **Listen to the description of the picture.** ((Track 235))

Speaking Practice

Pronunciation Practice

In casual speech, you may hear the word "or" pronounced as "er."

Written	Spoken
1. Do you live in a house or an apartment?	1. Do you live in a house er an apartment?
2. Should I put it in the closet or on the bed?	2. Should I put it in the closet er on the bed?
3. The apartments are furnished or unfurnished.	3. The apartments are furnished er unfurnished.

✓ **Now practice saying the following sentences.**

1. Try the door on the right or the one on the left.
2. Do you want to sit inside or outside?
3. You can rent a one-bedroom or two-bedroom.

✓ **Now listen and repeat.** ((Track 236))

B

Conversation Pictures

Listen to the dialogs, and number the pictures. ((Track 237))

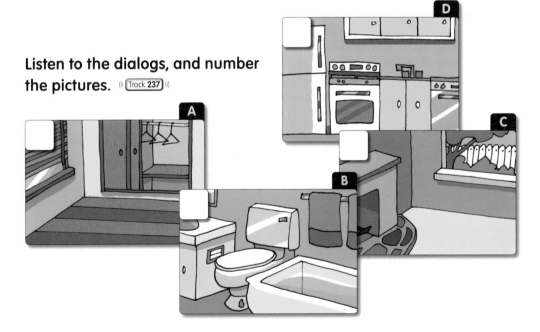

✓ **Now listen to the dialogs again, and choose the correct opinion of each room.**

1. (A) Small   (B) Large   2. (A) Small   (B) Large
3. (A) Small   (B) Large   4. (A) Small   (B) Large

Short Dialogs

A

Dialog 1

Listen to the dialog and questions. Choose the best answer. ((Track 238))

1. (A) An apartment
   (C) A dormitory
   (B) A condo
   (D) A house

2. (A) A beach
   (C) A park
   (B) A mall
   (D) A school

✓ Listen again, and fill in the blanks.

W: How big is your ❶_____?

M: It's a ❷_____ with a separate living room and ❸_____.

W: Is it close to the ❹_____?

M: Yes. It takes about ❺_____ minutes to walk from my apartment to ❻_____.

B

Dialog 2

Listen to the dialog and questions. Choose the best answer. ((Track 239))

1. (A) One
   (C) Three
   (B) Two
   (D) Four

2. (A) Bedrooms
   (C) Rooms
   (B) Beds
   (D) Doors

C

Dialog 3

Listen to the dialog, and complete each statement. ((Track 240))

1. He says that his parents' house is _____, but not really _____.

2. In their backyard, they have _____.

Main Dialog

Listen to the dialog, and choose the best answer. ((Track 241))

1. How long did he live in the dormitory?
   - (A) Two weeks
   - (B) One semester
   - (C) Two semesters
   - (D) Three years

2. What did he share with his roommate in the dorm?
   - (A) His closet
   - (B) His desk
   - (C) His room
   - (D) His TV

3. Which is probably true about the man and his roommate?
   - (A) They fought often.
   - (B) They had the same major.
   - (C) They were friends.
   - (D) They were not clean.

Listen again, and fill in the blanks. ((Track 242))

M: Wow, Denton Hall. This dormitory brings back memories.

W: Really? Did you live in a ❶_____ when you were in university?

M: Yes, I did for my first two ❷_____. After that, I left and moved into an ❸_____.

W: Why did you move out? You didn't like living in the ❹_____?

M: Well, it was alright. But I didn't really like sharing my ❺_____. I needed to have my own ❻_____.

W: Did you live ❼_____ after you moved into your apartment, or did you share it with someone?

M: Actually, my roommate from the dorm and I ❽_____ an apartment together. We liked living ❾_____, but we both wanted our own ❿_____.

W: Sometimes those dorm rooms can get a little cramped.

Short Talks

A
Short Talk 1

Listen to the short talk and questions. Choose the best answer. ((Track 243))

1. (A) One-bedroom   (B) Two-bedroom
   (C) One and two-bedroom   (D) None

2. (A) Elderly residents   (B) Single men
   (C) Students   (D) Young couples

✓ **Listen again, and fill in the blanks.**

Cedar Hills has three apartment options to choose from. We offer both one- and ❶_____ apartments that come unfurnished. We also offer ❷_____ furnished apartments that are popular with ❸_____ who choose to live here. Feel free to stop by our leasing ❹_____ any time if you'd like to ❺_____ the Cedar Hills ❻_____. No appointment is necessary.

B
Short Talk 2

Listen to the short talk and questions. Choose the best answer. ((Track 244))

1. (A) A brand new house   (B) A four-bedroom house
   (C) A two-story house   (D) A very old house

2. (A) Building it   (B) Cleaning it
   (C) Keeping it warm   (D) Selling it

C
Short Talk 3

Listen to the short talk, and number the events in order from 1-4. ((Track 245))

_____ (A) Lived in the dorm

_____ (B) Moved in to an apartment

_____ (C) Rented a house

_____ (D) Had his own room

Listening Quiz

A

Picture Matching

Listen to the dialogs. Choose the correct picture. ((Track 246))

1. (A)   (B)   (C)

2. (A)   (B)   (C)

B

Listen & Choose

Listen to the dialogs and questions. Choose the best answer. ((Track 247))

3. (A) The room is new.   (B) The room is not clean.
   (C) The room is small.   (D) The room is too warm.

4. (A) In an apartment   (B) In another country
   (C) On a farm   (D) Outside the city

5. (A) Buying a table   (B) Cleaning a room
   (C) Moving furniture   (D) Renting an apartment

6. (A) Away from the wall   (B) By the window
   (C) In another room   (D) Next to the wall

7. (A) Brothers   (B) Co-workers
   (C) Landlord and tenant   (D) Roommates

8. (A) Her coat   (B) The refrigerator
   (C) The television   (D) The toilet

9. (A) The one behind her   (B) The one at the end of the hall
   (C) The one on the left   (D) The one on the right

Wrap-up

Talk about these questions.

1. Do most of your relatives and friends live in houses or apartments?
2. Do you know anyone who lives in a house with a private pool? If yes, who?
3. Would you like to live somewhere with a private pool? Why or why not?

Listen and answer the questions. ((Track 248))

1. **If ten houses cost $250,000 each, how many of them probably have pools?**
   If ten houses cost $250,000 each, probably _____ of them have pools.

2. **What benefit can a homeowner expect from putting in a private pool?**
   The benefit that a homeowner can expect from putting in a private pool is _____
   _____
   _____ .

3. **What kinds of people usually live in homes with pools?**
   The kinds of people who usually live in homes with pools are _____
   _____ .

Listen again, and fill in the blanks. ((Track 249))

From movies and ❶_____, one might assume most ❷_____ in the United States ❸_____ pools. However, that is ❹_____ really true. Usually, only ❺_____ expensive homes have pools. ❻_____ to real estate statistics, ❼_____ all homes that cost ❽_____ million dollars or more ❾_____ a pool. Many of ❿_____ are indoor pools. For ⓫_____ that cost less, pools ⓬_____ not as common. In ⓭_____, less than 20 percent of ⓮_____ costing over $200,000 ⓯_____ a private swimming pool.

⓰_____ common misunderstanding about ⓱_____ pools is that pools ⓲_____ value to a house. ⓳_____, if a homeowner remodels ⓴_____ builds something to add ㉑_____ her or his home, the ㉒_____ of the property will go ㉓_____. This doesn't happen with ㉔_____. Actually, when homeowners sell ㉕_____ houses after building a ㉖_____ pool, they are lucky ㉗_____ they receive half of the ㉘_____ they spent to put ㉙_____ a pool. Therefore, homeowners ㉚_____ advised to only build ㉛_____ for enjoyment. They should ㉜_____ build them to make their ㉝_____ more valuable.

In the United States, ㉞_____ single people or families ㉟_____ school-aged children live in ㊱_____ with pools. Couples with ㊲_____ children and older people ㊳_____ to live in homes ㊴_____ pools. Pools are also ㊵_____ popular in the southwestern ㊶_____ of the country, where the ㊷_____ are longer and hotter.

Listening Test 🕓 08:53

PART I: Picture Description (((Track 250)))

Listen and choose the statement that best describes what you see in the picture.

1.

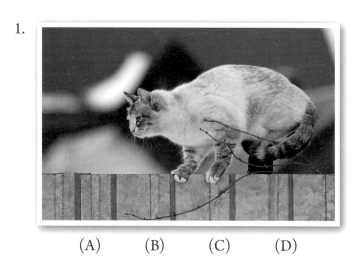

    (A)   (B)   (C)   (D)

2.

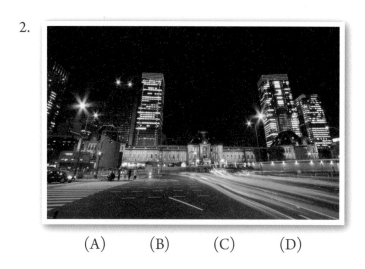

    (A)   (B)   (C)   (D)

3.

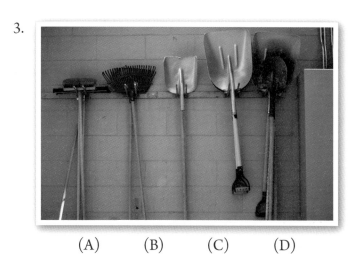

    (A)   (B)   (C)   (D)

4.

(A) (B) (C) (D)

5.

(A) (B) (C) (D)

PART II: Questions and Responses (Track 251)

Listen and choose the best response to each question.

6. (A)   (B)   (C)

7. (A)   (B)   (C)

8. (A)   (B)   (C)

9. (A)   (B)   (C)

10. (A)   (B)   (C)

PART III: Short Conversations ((Track 252))

You will hear two dialogs, each followed by three questions. Listen carefully, and choose the best answer to each question.

11. Where are the speakers?

    (A) A real estate agent's office
    (B) A hospital
    (C) A house
    (D) A bath house

12. Why is the backyard the woman's favorite place?

    (A) She likes sitting by the pool.
    (B) She enjoys gardening.
    (C) She wants to feed the birds.
    (D) She likes to spend her mornings there.

13. What does the woman usually do in the morning?

    (A) Go to the living room
    (B) Check her emails
    (C) Have a cup of coffee
    (D) Go jogging

---

14. Where did the man's parents live?

    (A) In the country
    (B) In another country
    (C) In a city
    (D) In the man's house

15. What did the woman assume about the man's mother?

    (A) She liked the house in the country.
    (B) She thought the countryside is too quiet.
    (C) She didn't like her husband.
    (D) She will decorate the house with new rugs.

16. What is true about the man's parents?

    (A) They moved to a smaller house.
    (B) They sold their old house downtown.
    (C) They have a new farm in the country.
    (D) His father doesn't like the peace and quiet there.

PART IV: Short Talks ((Track 253))

You will hear two talks, each followed by three questions. Listen carefully, and choose the best answer to each question.

17. What do dogs NOT do to gardens?

   (A) They eat fruit.
   (B) They make vegetables larger.
   (C) They make holes.
   (D) They crush flowers.

18. What is this advice for?

   (A) To hurt dogs
   (B) To protect gardens
   (C) To give melons to dogs
   (D) To get rid of gardens

19. Who is this advice for?

   (A) People with dogs
   (B) People with gardens
   (C) People with gardens and dogs
   (D) People who hate gardening

---

20. How many bedrooms does this house have?

   (A) One
   (B) Two
   (C) Three
   (D) Five

21. What kind of floor does this house have?

   (A) Wood
   (B) Wood and tile
   (C) Tile
   (D) Panels

22. What is an attractive feature of the house?

   (A) It's perfect for a large family.
   (B) It has two bedrooms and three bathrooms.
   (C) There is a nice mountain view from the bedroom.
   (D) It's very inexpensive.

Health

Warm-up

A
Look & Listen

Listen to the dialogs. ((Track 254))

B
Listen Again

Listen again, and fill in the blanks. ((Track 255))

1. She has belonged to the _____ for _____ months.
2. She exercises on the _____ between _____ minutes when she works out.
3. At his old gym, he did _____ every _____.
4. The gym requires new _____ to sign a _____ contract.

C
Essential Expressions

Sort the phrases into the right categories.

be out of shape	brush your teeth	catch a cold	do yoga
get a check-up	get food poisoning	go jogging	have a sore throat
have an X-ray	lift weights	work out	wrap it in a bandage

Exercise	Problems	Care/Treatment

Listening Practice

Listen. Write the answer. (((Track 256)))

No, I don't.	I think you're right.	No, I'm not tired.
Three kilometers.	Yes, it does.	

1. _____
2. _____
3. _____
4. _____
5. _____

Listen. Write the question. (((Track 257)))

When did you start doing yoga?	How about taking a break?
Where do you work out?	How do you feel?
Would you like some aspirin?	

1. _____
2. _____
3. _____
4. _____
5. _____

Describe the picture using the words below.

stethoscope	monitor	blood pressure	patient

_____
_____
_____
_____
_____

✓ **Listen to the description of the picture.** (((Track 258)))

Speaking Practice

A
Intonation Practice

In certain three-syllable statements or questions, the stress should be on either the first, second, or last syllable. Say the following statements and questions using the correct stress patterns.

Written	Spoken
1. How is it?	1. How **is** it?
2. Put it here.	2. Put it **here**?
3. Show me one.	3. **Show** me one.

✓ Now practice saying the following sentences. Remember to stress the first, second or last syllable.

1. How's your job?
2. What about you?
3. Look at that!

✓ Now listen and repeat. ((Track 259))

B
Conversation Pictures

Listen to the dialogs, and number the pictures. ((Track 260))

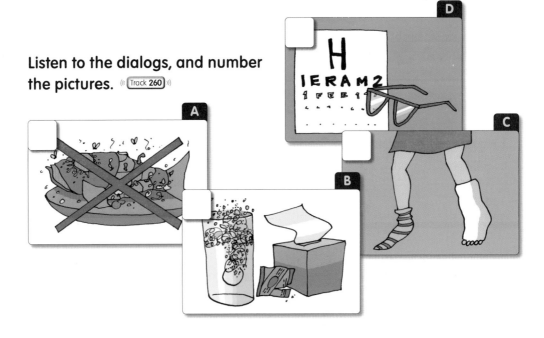

✓ Now listen to the dialogs again, and choose the correct time.

1. (A) Last night   (B) Last weekend   (C) Last Tuesday   (D) Last March
2. (A) Last night   (B) Last weekend   (C) Last Tuesday   (D) Last March
3. (A) Last night   (B) Last weekend   (C) Last Tuesday   (D) Last March
4. (A) Last night   (B) Last weekend   (C) Last Tuesday   (D) Last March

Short Dialogs

A

Dialog 1

Listen to the dialog and questions. Choose the best answer. ((Track 261))

1. (A) Lifting weights   (B) Playing tennis
   (C) Running   (D) Swimming

2. (A) He does not like exercise.   (B) He has never exercised before.
   (C) He is in better shape than her.   (D) He is in worse shape than her.

✓ **Listen again, and fill in the blanks.**

W: Do you want to jog around the ❶_____ one more time?

M: Sure, I think I can ❷_____ it one more time around.

W: If you're ❸_____, you can wait here for ❹_____. I know you haven't been ❺_____ in a while.

M: Don't worry about me. ❻_____ on, let's go.

B

Dialog 2

Listen to the dialog and questions. Choose the best answer. ((Track 262))

1. (A) Blood test   (B) Blood cells
   (C) Blood pressure   (D) Blood sugar

2. (A) Confused   (B) Happy
   (C) OK   (D) Worried

C

Dialog 3

Listen to the dialog, and match the right phrase. ((Track 263))

1. The man thinks   •   • (A) it might be a cold or allergies.

2. The woman thinks   •   • (B) it might be the flu.

Main Dialog

Listen to the dialog, and choose the best answer. (((Track 264)))

1. What sport did the man play?
   - (A) Basketball
   - (B) Golf
   - (C) Soccer
   - (D) Tennis

2. What is the problem with his hand?
   - (A) It has a cut on it.
   - (B) It is wrapped in a bandage.
   - (C) It is difficult to move.
   - (D) It was stepped on.

3. When might the man visit the doctor?
   - (A) In the evening
   - (B) Tomorrow
   - (C) Next week
   - (D) Never

Listen again, and fill in the blanks. (((Track 265)))

W: Hey, you don't look well. What happened to your ❶_____? It looks like it's swollen.

M: Oh, I hurt it playing ❷_____. It's still hurting me quite a bit.

W: That's too bad. I'm sorry to hear that. So, what happened? Did another player ❸_____ on your hand or something?

M: No. I ❹_____ the side of the goal by ❺_____ with my hand. Now I can't ❻_____ my little finger very well.

W: Well, if it's still hurting and you're having trouble moving your finger, maybe you ❼_____ get it X-rayed. You need to make sure that nothing is broken.

M: If it still hurts ❽_____ week, I think I will. But for ❾_____, I'll just keep it ❿_____ in a bandage.

Short Talks

A
Short Talk 1

Listen to the short talk and questions. Choose the best answer. (((Track 266)))

1. (A) A step in good brushing
   (C) How to brush your teeth
   (B) Choosing a good toothpaste
   (D) The best toothbrush to use

2. (A) Bad breath
   (C) Stained teeth
   (B) Gum disease
   (D) Tooth decay

✓ **Listen again, and fill in the blanks.**

One important ❶_____ many people forget when they brush their teeth is brushing their ❷_____. There are actually many germs and ❸_____ on the tongue. These can cause ❹_____. By just brushing with a regular ❺_____, these germs and bacteria can be eliminated. Some people buy special tongue ❻_____, but a regular toothbrush works just as well.

B
Short Talk 2

Listen to the short talk and questions. Choose the best answer. (((Track 267)))

1. (A) Aspirin
   (C) Cough medicine
   (B) Caffeine
   (D) Sleeping pills

2. (A) Basil
   (C) Red pepper
   (B) Parsley
   (D) Salt

C
Short Talk 3

Listen to the short talk, and write T for true or F for false for each sentence. (((Track 268)))

1. _____ She often swims for exercise.

2. _____ She doesn't jog because it is bad for her knees.

3. _____ She enjoys doing yoga.

Listening Quiz

Listen to the dialogs. Choose the correct picture. ((Track 269))

 A

 B

 C

1. (A)   (B)   (C)

2. (A)   (B)   (C)

Listen to the dialogs and questions. Choose the best answer. ((Track 270))

3. (A) Fighting   (B) Playing a sport
    (C) Watching a game   (D) Working out

4. (A) Enjoying free time   (B) Going to work
    (C) Racing   (D) Shopping

5. (A) A headache   (B) A neck ache
    (C) A runny nose   (D) A sore throat

6. (A) It didn't work.   (B) It was bitter.
    (C) It was expensive.   (D) It worked well.

7. (A) Doing math   (B) Going into a gym
    (C) Relaxing at home   (D) Stretching

8. (A) A clinic   (B) A gym
    (C) A pharmacy   (D) The man's house

9. (A) Coach   (B) Doctor
    (C) Housewife   (D) Nurse

Talk about these questions.

A

Pre-listening Discussion

1. How often do you take vitamin supplements?
2. What is vitamin C good for?
3. Do you think you get enough vitamin C each day? Why or why not?

B

Listening Comprehension

Listen and answer the questions. ((Track 271))

1. **How much vitamin C does a person need each day?**

   A person needs _____ of vitamin C each day.

2. **What is one problem a person might have if they take too much vitamin C?**

   If a person takes too much vitamin C, he or she might _____

   _____.

3. **What are good foods to eat to have enough vitamin C in your diet?**

   Good foods to eat in order to have enough vitamin C in your diet are

   _____.

C

Dictation Practice

Listen again, and fill in the blanks. ((Track 272))

Vitamin C is probably the ❶_____ popular vitamin that people ❷_____.
It is added to ❸_____. It is sold in ❹_____ tablets and candies. It is ❺_____
used to keep food ❻_____ longer. In the past, ❼_____ people got diseases
because ❽_____ did not have enough ❾_____ C in their diets. ❿_____,
these diseases are rare ⓫_____.

Doctors say people only need ⓬_____ milligrams of vitamin C per
⓭_____, and people can easily ⓮_____ this from normal foods. But
⓯_____ people still take vitamin C ⓰_____. They believe that
vitamin C ⓱_____ help prevent disease or even ⓲_____ colds. However,
these positive ⓳_____ of vitamin C have ⓴_____ been proven in research.
㉑_____ C is necessary for ㉒_____ health, but too much ㉓_____ C
can actually cause ㉔_____. People who take large ㉕_____ of this vitamin
may ㉖_____ from diarrhea or kidney ㉗_____. In addition, if people
㉘_____ large amounts for a ㉙_____ time and then stop, ㉚_____ may
become sick while ㉛_____ bodies adjust to lower ㉜_____ of vitamin C. Also,
㉝_____ vitamin C tablets can ㉞_____ the enamel on teeth. The ㉟_____ way
to make sure ㊱_____ get enough vitamin C ㊲_____ to eat fresh fruits ㊳_____
vegetables. Good sources of ㊴_____ C include oranges, ㊵_____,
tomatoes, and green ㊶_____.

Listening Test 🕗 08:48

PART I: Picture Description ((Track 273))

Listen and choose the statement that best describes what you see in the picture.

1.

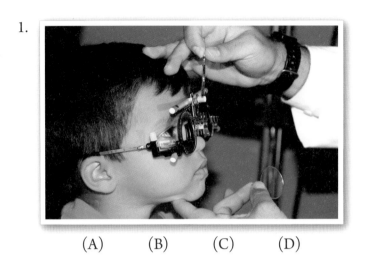

(A)   (B)   (C)   (D)

2.

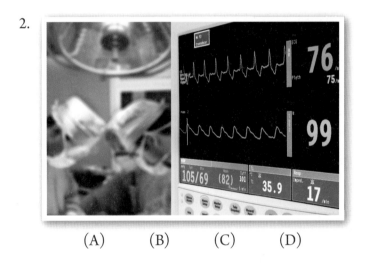

(A)   (B)   (C)   (D)

3.

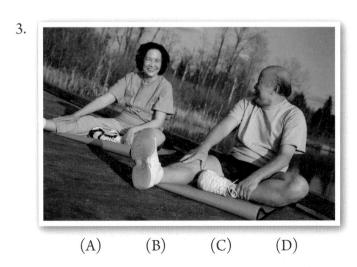

(A)   (B)   (C)   (D)

4.

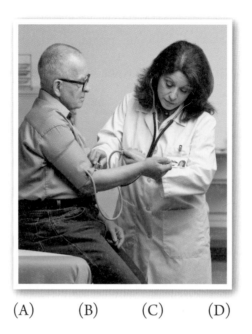

(A)   (B)   (C)   (D)

5.

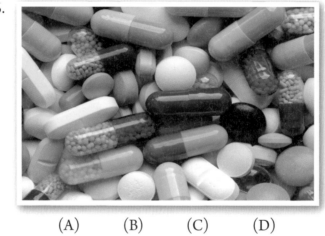

(A)   (B)   (C)   (D)

PART II: Questions and Responses (((Track 274)))

Listen and choose the best response to each question.

6. (A)   (B)   (C)

7. (A)   (B)   (C)

8. (A)   (B)   (C)

9. (A)   (B)   (C)

10. (A)   (B)   (C)

PART III: Short Conversations (((Track 275)))

You will hear two dialogs, each followed by three questions. Listen carefully, and choose the best answer to each question.

11. What type of exercise are they speaking about?

    (A) Weightlifting
    (B) Aerobics
    (C) Yoga
    (D) None of the above

12. Why didn't the man exercise?

    (A) Exercise is too hard.
    (B) The weather was bad.
    (C) It was too cold outside.
    (D) He could not make it.

13. Why did the man feel bad?

    (A) He was sick.
    (B) He had a terrible argument.
    (C) He was too tired.
    (D) He doesn't like to skip exercising for a day.

---

14. What was the man's opinion of the woman?

    (A) He does not like her.
    (B) He thinks she is funny.
    (C) He thinks her appearance is improving.
    (D) He thinks she should go on a vacation.

15. What does the man say about exercising?

    (A) It is healthy.
    (B) Three hours a day is too much.
    (C) It makes people very tired.
    (D) Exercising for fifteen minutes a day is enough.

16. What will the woman probably do tomorrow?

    (A) Exercise less
    (B) Not exercise
    (C) Try a different exercise routine
    (D) None of the above

MAY 0 1 2014

SEP 09 2014

428
Read

28 day

PART IV: Short Talks ((Track 276))

You will hear two talks, each followed by three questions. Listen carefully, and choose the best answer to each question.

17. Who is this advice for?

    (A) People who exercise
    (B) People who do not exercise
    (C) People who like easy exercise
    (D) People who plan to exercise

18. How can people hurt themselves?

    (A) By doing hard exercises too soon
    (B) By not exercising
    (C) By having a check-up
    (D) By walking

19. When should you start an exercise program?

    (A) Anytime
    (B) After doing easy exercises
    (C) After walking
    (D) After getting a check-up

20. What is special about green tea?

    (A) It is fresh.
    (B) You can drink a lot of it.
    (C) It is important for health.
    (D) It can help prevent cancer.

21. When is green tea most healthy?

    (A) When you drink it hot
    (B) When you drink five cups a day
    (C) When it is fresh
    (D) When it is served with ice

22. What did the announcement NOT say about green tea?

    (A) It's healthy.
    (B) The study was recent.
    (C) It is good for your dental health.
    (D) You must do certain things to get the benefits of green tea.